Wee
If you only h

MW00880924

All About

Java 8 Lambdas

Madhusudhan Konda

Author of *Just Spring* and *Just Hibernate*

DEDICATION

Dad, I miss you! We all miss you!

CONTENTS

FOREWORD

Without any doubt the release of Java 8 has firmly cemented Java as the world's most popular programming language. With the addition of Lambdas and the ability to manipulate data with streams, it has added powerful functional capabilities to its venerable base of Object Oriented features.

Sounds exciting doesn't it? But what do Lambdas and streams actually mean for your future and existing code bases? What are the fundamental traps and tricks you need to learn in order to use these new features effectively? What programming challenges are best solved with these new functional techniques? How on earth do you learn all of this complex material whilst doing your day job and juggling the rest of your life? These are all very valid questions!

Lambdas, streams and functional programming idioms represent a massive step change for most of the 9+ million Java developers out there today. In fact the concepts are so different that I found myself thinking for the first time "Is this still really Java? Will I be able to learn these new concepts and still count myself as a Java programmer?". It was actually quite a daunting set of changes which made me question my own abilities.

Luckily I was exposed to early builds of Java 8 and as part of the Adopt OpenJDK (http://adoptopenjdk.java.net) community programme. We ran several hack days and workshops with Brian Goetz (the lead engineer behind Lambdas at Oracle) at the London Java Community which allowed me to get comfortable with the new features over time. Of course most developers don't have that luxury of getting a year's head start, luckily this book is here to help!

I've had the pleasure of working with Madhu on various complex software problems during our days in Investment Banks. He excels in taking complex subject matters and distilling them into something that the rest of us can understand. As with his *Just Spring* and *Just Hibernate* titles, this book gets you over the hurdle of learning complex new technology and gets you tackling your coding problems using them with confidence on the following Monday.
If you want to get up to speed on Lambdas, streams and Java 8 quickly, then this is the book for you!

Martijn Verburg
"The Diabolical Developer"
CEO of jClarity, Java Champion, London Java Community Co-Leader

PREFACE

WHY I WROTE THIS BOOK

With so many new frameworks appearing every day and so little time to learn and master them, as a developer, I found it hard to catch up with the ever evolving world of programming. The programming jobs are demanding and fast paced often one needs to learn a language or a framework over a weekend and start coding the following Monday.

If only I found a book that would teach me everything I needed in a day or two.
A book that instils the required confidence to start coding immediately.

My aim is to deliver such books, a simple, straight-to-the-point and example driven books! A book that you should finish in a day or two! My dream is to write technical books that can be read over a weekend, and I sincerely hope this book accomplishes that dream!

I started my journey of writing books with the publication of *Just Spring*, the first book on the subject aimed at delivering a light read on Spring Framework. The book has been well-received (a new edition will be released in early 2016) and inspired me to write more. A great thanks to *you* all for the encouragement you have given me over the last few years.

I sincerely hope this book will be a good companion for your learning and understanding Java 8.

WHAT IS THIS BOOK ABOUT

Long due Java 8 is out here. It comes with a bang.

This book is about understanding Java 8 lambdas. Lambdas, are by far, the biggest changes introduced thus far in the language since it's inception. Along with lambdas, there are other features that come along - features such as interface unlocking, functional libraries, streams and parallelism to name a few. This book attempts to demystify these concepts in a plain and simple text with intuitive examples.

This book mainly concentrates on lambdas and other related concepts. There are features introduced in Java 8 such as new Time and Date and Time, Nashorn Scripting etc, which will not be covered in this book.

You must have an understanding of Java programming language. This book does not teach you how to program in Java.

WHERE IS THE CODE

This Book accompanies Java code project. The code is available on my Github here: https://github.com/madhusudhankonda/AllAboutLambdas. I will be updating the codebase as and when required and if you have any suggestions or recommendations, or wish to contribute, do get in touch with me. I will sincerely appreciate if you can contribute to the repository.

I tried to keep the code snippets very concise as to not to loose the focus of the concept that it was meant for. For brevity and to keep the concept crisp, I have excluded presenting full working programs in the code blocks. This way, you won't be distracted from unnecessary code blocks when reading the book. I expect you to checkout the project from the repository when going in hands on mode.

WHO AM I INDEBTED TO

There are few people who reviewed, ratified, explained, inspired and encouraged through out the time of writing. I am truly indebted to all of them.

I wish to express my sincere gratitude Dr. Sue Greene for her tremendous help in reviewing the book. Without her unending and unbounded help, I would not have accomplished this project.

I also wish to express my sincere thanks to Author, LJC founder, Java Evangelist, CEO of jClarity and a good friend Martijn Verburg, who agreed to write the foreword in spite of his extremely busy schedules.

I also wish to express my gratitude to Mani Sarkar, working for Codurance, an active member of LJC, for instantly agreeing to review the book. His eye-to-detail is commendable and his detailed review enhanced sections of book very much. He has happily agreed to share his code repo, which is here: https://github.com/neomatrix369/LambdaExamples.

Also, my sincere thanks to Simon Maple, Head of Developer Advocacy, ZeroTurnaround, founder of VirtualJUG and co-leader of London JUG, who reviewed the book patiently and rendered gentle recommendations. I would also wish to thank my friend and Istanbul JUG leader, Rahman Usta, who helped me in improving the text by spotting technical errors.

I wish to express my sincere thanks to Arun Gupta and Sharat Chandra for their inputs and recommendations.

I render my sincere gratitude to Mark Swindell for his invaluable suggestions. His meticulous pointers helped me enhance the material. I also thank Bartosz Jankiewicz for providing me pointers for future edition.

There are many of my friends who encouraged me, stood by me and supported in numerous ways. I am grateful to Ravi Sarikonda, Vijay Kumar, Praveen EGK, Krishnababu Marella, Ajay Kumar Sathuluri, Sumit Mukherji, Somay Nakhal and many others for their inputs in making this book see limelight.

If there's one person that I cannot thank enough - that's my darling wife! She has been the beacon through out this project, being there when needed, encouraging me and guiding me when lost, looking after my well being and understanding when I skip the household chores! I can't forget mentioning the unbound love of my 9 year son Joshua for me as his 'Author Dad'. He is the inspiration in writing simple books. He made me realise keeping things simple is far more difficult!

Lastly, I am truly thankful to *you* all for the your support and time in reading my books. I am really grateful to you for encouragement, which motivates me to write more. Each email that arrives in my inbox mentioning you are reading the book or a tweet that says the book helped you (or even a mistake you found) are so uplifting and go long way!

CONTACTING ME

I love writing, be it a simple article or an elaborative book or even fiction. I enjoy writing books, technical papers, mentoring, reviews and of course speaking at seminars/webinars. As an Indian living in the UK, I do my best to avoid *Indian* English in the text, but unfortunately it flows inevitably!

Not everyone will like this book, but I do love to hear from everyone of you! Your feedback is invaluable and only makes me better next time. If you are interested in a seminar/hands on courses/mentoring or even enjoying a cup of coffee with me, please do get in touch. If you are in London or planning to be in London sometime, ping me, perhaps we can go for a coffee!

I am easily accessible either email or twitter: m.konda@outlook.com or @mkonda007 or visit my website www.madhusudhan.com

HOW THIS BOOK IS ORGANISED

This book reveals the concepts like a story, straight to the point and without much of distractions. The code examples in this book are deliberately chosen to be simple and basic. All the examples are available online at the book's Github location (see *where is the code* section above).

Each code example will have a Java class file name followed by the method name where appropriate, like: `Runnables.java#usingLambda,` for example. Where necessary, I have marked important notes in side boxes, do go over them without fail. The full source code is available on the github, so checkout and play with it. More than happy if you commit improvements!

COVER DESIGN

The cover page and the Harp is designed and developed by my wife and my son. Harp is an ancient multi-stringed musical instrument dating back 3500 BC. It is a key instrument of the medieval age, thought to have had their origins from a hunter's bow. Beautifully carved with varying lengths of strings producing rich sounds, it is said that Harp's music soothes the soul!

1. INTRODUCTION

Java 8 brings a breath of fresh air to the language landscape. Touted to be a game changer, it embraces the functional programming style. Lambda expressions, evolution of interfaces, overhauled libraries, data processing support using streams and out-of-the-box parallelism are some of the the biggest changes introduced thus far in the language since its inception. Java started falling behind in its peer groups and hence bringing the language up to date will certainly win developers heart, who waited patiently declaring their allegiance to Java for almost two decades.

Before we delve into details, let us get a birds view of lambda expressions using basic examples.

Birds View

It's a common saying that Men don't read manuals! If that's anything to go by, we wish to look at lambdas in action rather than reading few chapters praising them. Some of the functionality may baffle you at first, but trust me, this book should be your best companion in demystifying the language features.

Runnable Example

Working with `Runnables` is straight forward and I am sure you may have created and executed threads using `Runnables` umpteen times. Say we have to run some errands at home while watching a movie. The `runErrands` method is expected to be executed in a separate thread, hence we create a `Runnable` implementation wrapping the `runErrands` method and ask a new `Thread` to execute it. There are three approaches in achieving this - let's start exploring those approaches.

Using `Runnable` Instance

In this approach, we follow a traditional method of creating an instance of a `Runnable` and asking the `Thread` to invoke it.

This is demonstrated in the code snippet here below:

```
// Runnables.java#instanceRunnable

// Concrete implementation of Runnable
Runnable oldRunnable = new Runnable() {
  @Override
  public void run() {
    System.out.println("Errands using traditional Runnable!");
    runErrands();
  }
};

//Execute the Runnable
new Thread(oldRunnable).start();
```

In order to run our business logic (i.e., `runErrands`), we have created an implementation of the `Runnable` interface and invoked the logic in the `run` method. We then created a `Thread` passing our `Runnable` to execute. Apart from invoking the `runErrands` method, the other five lines of code are non-business related (boiler plate) code.

Using Anonymous Class

The other way to kickstart the thread is using an *anonymous* class approach. Here, we do not instantiate a `Runnable` instance instead create the anonymous class inline, as demonstrated here:

```
// Runnables.java#anonymousRunnable

// Runnable as anonymous class
new Thread(new Runnable(){
  @Override
  public void run() {
    System.out.println("Using an Anonymous runnable");
    runErrands();
  }
});
```

Comparing with the first approach, the boiler plate code exists in this approach too. Apart from saving to create an instance variable, there's not much of a structural difference between both of these approaches. In either of the cases (instance or anonymous class approaches), our business logic (of running errands) is obscure and hidden away under the boiler plate code.

Using Lambda Expression

Well, not going too much in detail, the above logic can be expressed as a *lambda expression,* as shown below:

```
// Runnables.java#usingLambda

// Create a lambda expression
Runnable runErrandsLambda = () -> runErrands();

// Ask the thread be execute the lambda
new Thread(runErrandsLambda).start();
```

We created our first lambda expression assigning it to the Runnable which calls business logic (runErrands), throwing away all the fluff around. The code is not only clear and concise, the intent of the business logic is very clearly explained. Instead of creating an instance of a Runnable using the lambda expression (as we did in the above example), we can create a lambda inline, as shown here:

```
// Runnables.java#usingLambda

// The lambda expression is created inline
new Thread(() -> {
  System.out.println("Using a Lambda Expression");
  listErrands();
  runErrands();
}).start();
```

The Thread is now receiving a code expression that encompasses the printing of a debug statement, listing the errands and finally running the errands. There's no instance of Runnable created in this invocation (however, the expression must adhere to Runnable interface definition - more later).

For brevity, let me show you the full example here (checkout the code from github for the full working programs mentioned in this book):

```
// Runnables.java#usingLambda

public class Runnables {
  public static void main(String[] args) {
    Runnables client = new Runnables();
    client.usingLambda();
  }
  public void usingLambda() {
    // Simple lambda expression
    Runnable runnableLambdaSimple = () -> runErrands();
    new Thread(runnableLambdaSimple).start();

    // Lambda expression created inline
    new Thread(() -> {
      listErrands();
      runErrands();
    }).start();
  }
}
```

Now if you wish to sit and relax rather than running errands, changing your mode is as easy as a Sunday morning:

```
// Runnables.java#usingLambda

new Thread(() -> stayRelax()).start;
```

In the above lambda, we are passing the lambda expression directly to the Thread. This is nothing but passing code just the way we pass data, which was impossible prior to Java 8 (passing methods to methods is not allowed up until Java 8).

This chapter would not be complete if we did not mention streams. Streams are another new addition to the language used for data processing on continuous stream of data. We will check out briefly an example using streams here, but note that I have dedicated a good part of this book to Streams.

Streaming Example

Consider a requirement of employing some data processing techniques on data., for example, fetching a list of big trades given a list of trades. Without going too much detail, here is the snippet of the code that does this job:

```
// Streaming.java#findLargeTrades

// Stream through the trades, filtering non-big ones
trades.stream()
  .filter(trade -> trade.getQuantity() > ONE_MILLION)
  .forEach(System.out::println);
```

The above code uses streaming techniques on the source, filtering unwanted trades based on the big-trade-condition. The code is simple, expressive, no iterations or no temporary storage variables.

A stream is nothing but a free flowing sequence of elements following a pipeline architecture (pipes and filters pattern). Every stream starts with a source of data, sets up a pipeline, processes the elements through a pipeline using intermediate operators and finishes with a terminal operation. The terminal operators are the final components that produce a result at which point stream comes to cease.

Running the code parallelly on available cores (multi-core processing) couldn't be any easier:

```
//Streaming.java#findLargeTradesInParallel

// Run the operations in parallel mode
List<Trade> bigTrades = trades
   .stream()
   .parallel()
   .filter(t -> t.isBigTrade())
   .collect(toList());
```

We did not create a load of classes or complex infrastructure for the execution of the program in a parallell mode. We did not burn code in getting the fork/join framework ready or managing the jobs or sub-jobs. Instead we simply invoked a method (parallel) on the stream and the job is done! Parallellism without hassle is what we are getting in Java 8. However, note that switching a slow running program to parallel mode (because it is easy to switch!) doesn't mean the program is going to yield results at a supersonic speed. There are consequences when parallelism is sought, one must understand the problem domain thoroughly and measure the gains (or losses) before diving into changing sequential processing to a parallel fashion.

Stream is a flow of data elements drawn from a source, through a pipeline, with operations such as transformation, mapping, filtering being applied on the elements.

The syntax of a lambda expression or streams might be a bit unusual, but trust me, it's no more complicated than assembling simple lego. Before we close this section on lambdas, let me shown you few more lambda expressions here for completeness:

```java
// Examples.java

// A Callable lambda expression performing various operations
//on a given Trade

Callable<Trade> c = () -> {
  Trade t = new Trade( "GOOGLE", 2000, "OPEN");
  encrypt(t);
  persist(t);
  return t;
};

// A parallel streaming pipeline summing up the total quantity
// of all trades

trades
  .stream()
  .parallel()
  .map(Trade::getQuantity)
  .reduce(Integer::sum);

// Fetching distinct movies of Spielberg
movies
  .stream()
  .filter(m-> m.getDirector().equals("Steven Spielberg"))
  .map(Movie::getName)
  .distinct()
  .forEach(System.out::println);
```

We will run through the details of creating and working lambdas in coming chapters but in the mean time let's study the forces behind Java 8 upgrade, the reasons an Object Oriented language embracing Functional programming style (perhaps, becoming a functional and object oriented language (*FOO*))!

Forces

Few things in life force us to change or at least make us adapt to change. Likewise, in my opinion, there are three main forces acted together to drive the change in Java landscape. Let us briefly examine those forces here. Of course, there are other factors too, but for simplicity, we consider the following three main forces.

Processing Power

Even a simple tablet or a phone gadget nowadays comes with multi-core processing chips onboard. The powerful cores can be put to effective use by employing parallel mode executions. Incredible advances in computer processing power over the last two decades pushed Java language to the edge. A programming language can only flourish if it can harness the power of parallel computing with a feature rich tool kit and well suited functions.

Java, with its age old libraries and cumbersome multi-core programming styles, was lagging behind. While other languages embraced the advances in technological power, Java trailed back due to a plethora of reasons. While they strive to be more precise and concise, Java made no considerable attempts in this direction. There is also a steep rise of big data applications over the last few years. The use of big data in private and public sectors with the demand for churning large volumes of data is growing exponential.

Java was no doubt a great platform for server side applications but designing and developing multi-processor applications is still a dreaded job. Developer needs to deal with the nitti-gritties of working with low level threading and memory models when developing concurrent and parallel applications. Threading makes even seasoned programmers nervous. To embrace the challenges posed due to the exponential growth in multi-core humongous machines, it was imperative to reengineer the language, introduce modern toolkits and libraries for supporting such challenges.

Capturing Behaviour

Capturing behaviour and passing it around like data is the crux of functional programming paradigm. We call this *code as data,* that is, passing a block of program code representing behaviour. This feature is not new to Java, it exists in the form of anonymous class strategy, however working with anonymous class is annoyance and certainly comes with wrinkles. Due to their verbosity, tight coupling and scope resolution, anonymous classes soon became non-programmer friendly. They carry unnecessary baggage as well as complex rules making the code unfortunately untidy.

Java class represents state and behaviour as class variables and methods respectively, but the methods are not designed to accept another method as its argument. That is, we cannot pass a method to another method. Capturing functional behaviour and passing it around as data was another big challenge.

Overhauling Libraries

The final force came from the need to enhance the application libraries without creating chaos. Any programming language thrives on its good design and usage of its libraries. Over time, the libraries needs to be enhanced to factor in the changing landscape and requirements. Hence, libraries are expected to be ever evolving.

The heart of any framework is a humble interface definition. As we know, the interfaces up until Java 8 were pretty much written in stone. Once they are made public, they can not be changed unless we break backward compatibility. Enhancing these libraries without hurting the developer community is a herculean task. The ideal choice was to reengineer and update the libraries rather than reinventing the wheel.

Birth of Java 8

As Java Designers wished for these three wishes, a *Genie* appeared and gave them all in one go - in the form of Lambdas! Well, sort of. Lambdas are the newest addition to the language, corner stone to the language's modernisation. No doubt, Java 8 is the greatest milestone in the history of Java so far.

To conclude, Java 8 is a boat that one shouldn't miss. In my opinion, the language is evolving with a bang in a right direction. The revolution has just begun, it will continue into Java 9 and to possibly into future versions too.

Summary

This chapter introduced the problem domain and helped us to understand the need for Java 8. We looked at various factors that may have contributed to Java 8's birth such as emerging ease of computing power, parallel programming and the need for enhancing the age old libraries. Without delving too much into lambda expressions, we looked at few examples of how lambdas can change the course of Java programming world, holding our hands to functional universe.

2. NEW FEATURES

Java 8 introduced lambda expression, and with it came many new features. In addition to lambdas, Java 8 has a considerable list of achievements: interfaces unlocked, libraries overhauled, streaming introduced, parallel programming simplified to name a few. In this chapter we explore the new features at a glance.

Lambdas

The fusion of Object orientated programming language with functional style (a Functional and Object Oriented (FOO) language!) has enormous advantages. Programs become more expressive with richer code, shorter and less error prone encouraging behaviour parameterisation and immutability as well as supporting the modern computer architectures. Java 8 was successful in supporting long standing wish list of using functions in Java.

Lambdas lead to better programming style. The behaviour can be parameterised quite concisely with lambdas. The clumsiness of using anonymous classes is history and elegance of writing functional code is the future.

Functional programming is all about maintaining immutable state in a function, returning the same output for the same input. A function is treated as a first class citizen and is free from side-effects.

Lambdas enable the concept of lazy iterations built into library. A client doesn't need to worry about how to slice and dice a huge dataset, but simply instructs the program what to do. Developers don't need to deal with *how* to do the iteration instead simply instruct the framework *what* to do.

Here's a `Tradable` interface for checking various conditions and the relevant lambda expressions:

```java
// TradableLambda.java

// Functional interface for checking a trade
interface Tradable<Trade>{
  boolean check(Trade t);
}
// Lambda expressions checking various conditions
// Check for a large transaction
Tradable<Trade> bigTradeLambda = (t)-> t.isBigTrade();

// Is the trade in a cancelled state?
Tradable<Trade> cancelledLambda = (t)-> t.isCancelledTrade();

// Is the trade new or unknown?
Tradable<Trade> newOrUnknownTrade = (t)-> {
 return
    t.getStatus().equals("NEW")||
    t.getStatus().equals("UNKNOWN");
}
```

These are the free floating code expressions that can be passed around like data. They are instrumental in parameterising the behaviour. Note that the same functionality of conditional checking is provided by library in the name of `Predicate` function so we don't need to create functional interfaces for common cases. We will run through the functional interfaces in due course.

Interfaces

In Java, interface is a static definition and certainly opens up pandora box of issues related to backward compatibility if changes to the interface definition are introduced. Once an interface is made into a library, changing the interface has repercussions.

With Java 8, interfaces have been redesigned and redefined. Now, we can change the definitions of existing interfaces without having to worry about backward compatibility. We add concrete implementations of methods to the interfaces encouraging default definitions and initialisation code. We can modify and release the newer versions of the interfaces with no implications for the older library users.

For example, consider the definition of the interface `Component` below, which has a single abstract method `getName` and two fully implemented methods getDefaultName and getRegion. Prior to Java 8, we wouldn't have been able to add these concrete implementations to an interface.

```java
// Component.java

// Unlocked interface - no longer an abstract!
@FunctionalInterface
public interface Component {
  // One abstract method (so it can represent a lambda)
  String getName();

  // Fully implemented default method
  default String getDefaultName(){
    return "Default Component";
  }

  // Fully implemented static method
  static String getRegion(){
    return "United Kingdom";
  }
}
```

Notice that the concrete methods declared must either be of a static or default type. The compiler will moan if you provide neither of the classifiers. Also, note the declaration of the annotation @FunctionalInterface on the interface. Although optional, the annotation will safeguard from the inappropriate use of a functional interface. We will learn a lot more about interfaces including static and default methods in the coming chapters.

Default and Static methods

As we noted earlier, Java 8 opened the doors for interface unlocking. We can now create default and static methods to an interface. We can of course modify the existing interfaces too should the need arise (and hence the reason why Java 8 interfaces such as Runnable, Callable, Comparator etc were retrofitted). The method should be prefixed by default or static keywords appropriately, providing the full implementation of logic in the interface.

If you check the Comparator interface definition (see Javadoc), you will find a handful of default and static methods are added in Java 8 version.

Functional Interfaces

A functional interface has one abstract method, and hence can be used as a target type of a lambda expression. Wherever we have a functional interface as an input type to a method, it can be substituted with a lambda expression.

Thereby, lambdas and functional interfaces go hand in hand!

```
// Finder.java

@FunctionalInterface
public interface IFinder {

  // Abstract method
  String find(String criteria);

  // default method
  default String criteria(){
    return "Search criteria:";
  }
}
```

The IFinder interface has one abstract method and a concrete default method. As long as we define only one abstract method, this interface can be classified as a functional interface and hence can act as the target type for a lambda expression.

The lambda expression is shown in the following code snippet, note the target type of the lambda:

If the interface has only one abstract method, irrespective of other default or static methods, it becomes a candidate to stand in as a type for a lambda expression. This interface has a special name called *functional interface*.

```
// Lambda expression using the above functional interface
IFinder finder = (input) -> "output result";
```

Functions

Functions are recurring patterns that we use when developing applications. Java 8 provides a set of function definitions as a library rather than us creating and sprinkling them all over the place. A new package java.util.function was introduced for this purpose. Functions help achieve a consistent way of designing artefacts.

Functions such as Predicate, Consumer, Supplier are readily available from the functions library. For that matter, even specialised functions such as IntPredicate, LongPredicate, or DoublePredicate (there are handful of such specializations such as IntConsumer, DoubleConsumer, IntFunction, DoubleFunction etc) are available straight off the shelf. Our previous example of finding out the the large trade or a big trade can be re-written using a Predicate function which is part of standard Java 8 library, as shown in the following code example:

```
// Check for a big trade
Predicate<Trade> bigTradeLambda =(t)-> t.isBigTrade();

// Predicate for checking a cancelled trade
Predicate<Trade> cancelledLambda = (t)-> t.isCancelledTrade();

// Predicate checking for new or unknown trade
Predicate<Trade> newOrUnknownTrade = (t)-> {
  return
  t.getStatus().equals("NEW")||
  t.getStatus().equals("UNKNOWN");
};
```

The above lambda expressions have been assigned to a Predicate type to check the conditionality of the various criteria. The Predicate is a library function that ideally should replace any of our custom made predate-conditional-checking functions. There are a couple of chapters dedicated for learning functions in the coming chapters.

Streams

Streams are yet another big stride in Java 8 language. It's a new concept introduced to deal effectively with big data analytical operations. Simply put, stream is a sequence of elements. While Collections are standard data structures for storing and accessing data, streams on the hand do not hold any storage but manipulate or analyse the data as per the predefined business logic. Adding streams greatly simplifies the collection libraries and enable big-data operations efficiently.

Streams complements lambda expressions. With the help and support from lambda expressions, streams delivers a powerful collections library. Take an example of finding out list of classics from a huge collection of movies, using streams:

```
//StreamsFeature.java#findClassics

return movies
   .stream()
   .filter(m -> m.isClassic())
   .collect(toList());
```

This code is much more expressive and fluent! It says once we *streamify* the movies, we filter them out using the classic movie predicate and collect them to a list.

Parallel Operations

Utilising the full processing power of a computer leads to a big win. Streams along with lambdas help creating parallel programs and lazy evaluations with ease and comfort. Lazy evaluations allow programs to wire up the sequence of operations but will not execute them until an event is triggered. Streams help filtering, mapping and slicing of data both in sequential as well as parallel mode. It is only the beginning to a joyful ride.

Turning a sequential program to a parallel is matter of changing a simple method call. We can enable parallelism really easy unlike in earlier versions of Java, where we have to deal with low level mechanics of threading and concurrency.

For example, if our collection has millions of movies, it would be a pretty easy to run the program in parallel without stretching a muscle. Simply invoke a method called `parallel` on the stream to let the operations run parallelly, effectively using the multiple cores of the machine.

The following code snippet demonstrates an example of collecting classic movies by running the program in a parallel mode:

```
// ParallelStreamsFeature.java

// Collecting Classic Movies using parallel program
return movies.stream()
  .parallel()
  .filter(m -> m.isClassic())
  .collect(toList());

// Or, using the parallelStream on the collection
return movies
  .parallelStream()
  .filter(m -> m.isClassic())
  .collect(toList());
```

Invoking the `parallel` (or `parallelStream`) method make the pipeline of operations run in a parallel mode - thus utilising the processing power.

Other Features

In addition to the above fundamental language features, Java 8 also introduced a new Time and Date API.

If you ever worked with Date and Time in Java, I'm sure you would agree that it was pain in the neck. It's the most unfriendly and complicated API which was almost universally hated by the Java developer community. An opersource alternative called *Joda Time API* emerged to relieve us from the peril. In the mean time, fortunately, Java designers listened to the criticism and hence on-boarded a new Date and Time API by drawing a lot of inspiration and design from Joda Time. The newly created `java.time` package hosts date and time components.

Another prominent feature in Java 8 is the scripting support for Javascript engine Nashorn. Java 8 marked the end of Rhino as its scripting engine and brought in Nashorn, a JavaScript scripting engine. Nashorn works via `invokeDynamic` site facility introduced in Java 7, and of course comes with greater gains in the performance area.

Note that the Date and Time API along with the Nashorn scripting engine is not in the scope for this book.

Summary

This chapter is a whirlwind pass at the new features of Java 8. We looked at the features of the language from a very high level with examples where possible. We introduced ourselves to lambdas, functional interfaces, functions as well as explored the streams very briefly.

3.INTRODUCING LAMBDAS

Java is an Object oriented programming language. Methods and variables are tied to a class and the class must be instantiated before invoking the methods to execute the functions appropriately. We cannot have a variable or a block of code that does not belong to a Class.

Class is the fundamental structure, even if it's a single line of business logic, it must be written in a method and declared in a class. With the advent of Java 8, we can write blocks of code and pass them to other methods as if we are passing the data. A class used to be the first class citizen in Java, however, with the introduction of lambdas, the smallest unit of code is a lambda!

This chapter is all about demystifying the lambdas and trying to understand the bigger picture.

What are Lambdas?

Lambdas are blocks of program code that represents behaviour similar to a function. It can be passed around to other methods just as we pass data – hence we say code as data. They are anonymous functions and are concise, clean and expressive. They are sort of free floating code blocks helping us write *functional code*.

Consider the following examples:

```java
// LambdaTasters.java

// Lambda printing out a Quote each day
Quote quoteLambda =
  ( ) -> System.out.println("Hello, Lambdas!");

// The functional interface definition:
interface Quote{
  void quoteOfTheDay();
}
```

This is a simple lambda expression which, when invoked prints out the quote to the console. Don't worry if it doesn't make any sense. All you need to know at this point is that it does something (printing out a message to the console) given no arguments.

Similarly, take another example of a lambda expression that extract the trade's instrument:

```
// LambdaTasters.java

// Lambda fetching the instrument of a Trade
Instrument<Trade> instrumentLambda =
  (t)-> t.getInstrument();

// Functional interface defintion:
interface Instrument<T>{
  String extract(T t);
}
```

In both examples, we have a functional interface and a lambda expression defined. As you can see from the lambda expressions, they are new to us and they have a special syntax and semantics.

Lambdas are in essence mathematical functions. They map their input to a unique output, including the case of an empty parameter list. They represent behaviour, behaviour such as to reserve a seat on a flight, convert the temperature from Centigrade to a Fahrenheit, merging two trades, or aggregating the entire wealth of high net worth individuals. We can use lambdas to parameterise this sort of functional behaviour.

Using lambdas we can model ever changing client requirements with ease and comfort.

Lambdas are anonymous functions representing program behaviour. We can pass them just as we pass data to a method

Strictly speaking lambdas are not free floating code blocks but are functions implementing a special interface called functional interface. The functional interface must have one and only one abstract method defined.

Problem Domain

The best way to learn lambda feature is work through an example.

Let's take some requirements such as checking if the given trade needs encryption, does it need to be offloaded due its associated market risk or is it a large transaction that can be spilt up etc. Usually, we design and define an interface to capture and execute such behaviours. As we have already created an interface called `Tradable` with an abstract method `check(T t)` in our earlier chapters, we can use it as our base for understanding and dissecting the lambda's signature and syntax.

The definition of the interface is shown below once again for completeness:

```
// DissectingLambda.java

// Functional interface for checking characteristics
interface Tradable<T>{
  boolean check(T t);
}
```

Now that we have a functional interface, we can develop few lambda expressions for variety of cases. Say, we wish to check if the trade is large, we create a lambda expression with appropriate business logic as demonstrated in the code snippet below:

```
// Big trade lambda expression
Tradable<Trade> bigTradeLambda = (t) -> t.isBigTrade();
```

The right hand side of the assignment is a lambda expression. It says given a `Trade t`, invoke `isBigTrade` method to return a `boolean` result (we will learn about the syntax real soon).

The type of a lambda expression is a functional interface and hence the above lambda is assigned to a variable of type `Tradable<Trade>`.

Here, we are creating an instance of `Tradable` with a lambda expression associated to it.

However, instead of creating a lambda and assigning it to a type, we can instead pass the lambda expression directly to any method that accepts the `Tradable<Trade>` as parameter, like the `checkCharecteristics` method shown here in this snippet:

```
// DissectingLambda.java#checkCharecteristics

// Passing a lambda expression to the method
private void checkCharecteristics(Tradable<Trade>
lambda, Trade t){
  tradableLambda.check(trade);
}
```

The method accepts a functional interface, thus abstracting the logic so clients can pass in several lambda expressions suited to their own requirements, as demonstrated here:

```
// Create the instances
DissectingLambda client = new DissectingLambda();
Trade trade = new Trade(..);

// Is the trade in cancelled state?
client.checkCharecteristics
  ((t) -> t.isCancelledTrade(), trade);

// Is it a risky trade
client.checkCharecteristics
  ((t)-> client.isRisky(), trade);
```

As you may have noted, the checkCharecteristics method is capable of receiving code expression that sticks to a specified signature: *given a Trade, return a boolean value*. In both the examples, we are declaring the lambda code inline and passing it to the checkCharecteristics method. Thus, we are delivering the required behaviour without having to duplicate code. Client has more flexibility to create the behaviour.

We broadly understood the lambda it is time to understand the special syntax lambda has.

Syntax

Consider the following lambda expression we had seen earlier:

```
// Lambda expression printing a message
( ) → System.out.println("Hello, Lambdas!");
```

The syntax may first seem a bit baffling. It is something we are not used to in Java language so far. There is a special syntax representing a lambda expression. But it is not too dissimilar to what a Java method is, except that

19

its representation is a bit different.

Lambda Constituents

The syntax of a lambda expression is derived from the functional interface definition. Similar to a normal method, lambda has input arguments and a body, a return value and possibly an exception. It is easy to grasp the syntax when we look at it from a method perspective.

To keep things simple, we can split the lambda expression into two parts: left hand and right hand parts. The parts are separated using an arrow token ($\rightarrow$) in between. The left part of this arrow is holder of input arguments to the lambda expression while the right side part is the body of the lambda. Body is where we apply business logic and return a result, void if nothing to return.

> Lambda syntax is simple and follows the footsteps of a method. It has input parameters, body and return statement along with exceptions if any.

When creating a lambda expression, we take the input parameters on the left hand side and the body on the right hand side, separated by an arrow as demonstrated in the following code snippet:

```
// Highlevel lambda expression
(Input arguments) → { body }
```

Let's compare this syntax with our earlier example to pick the right pieces from the expression:

```
( ) → System.out.println("Hello, Lambdas!");
```

The left hand side is where the arguments are presented, in this case the lambda has an empty parenthesis, meaning *no* input arguments are expected by this lambda. The right hand side is the body representing the business logic, printing a message in this case. The body is a simple print statement returning void and no exceptions declared.

If we have only one parameter, the parenthesis is optional, the argument list becomes even simpler, as shown here below:

```
// Single parameter, see next snippet what we can do
(Trade t) -> t.getInstrument().equals("IBM")

// Drop the parenthesis and type!
t -> t.getInstrument().equals("IBM")
```

Deducing the types

In the lambda expression t -> t.getInstrument().equals("IBM"), the input parameter is not declared with a type. Obviously, the Java compiler should ideally be unhappy by looking at this. However, we can ignore the type of the input parameters as they are *inferred* by the compiler from the functional interface's definition. The compiler can deduce that t is indeed a Trade type. We will run through target typing and type inference in due course.

Return values

Declaration of a return value from the lambda's body is interesting. The return type is explicit in some cases where we must declare the value output. Other cases it is implicit, in which case the return value is omitted. Look at the following lambda expression:

```
// DissectingLambda.java
// Lambda expression for a cancelled trade

// return is implicit
(t) -> t.isCancelledTrade()
```

We did not declare a return value in the body of the expression shown above because, as this is a simple expression, the output is implicitly returned to the caller. That is, we can ignore attaching a return keyword if the body is a statement or a simple expression.

However, if we have a bit of complex block of code block with various control paths, then we have to explicitly mark the return.

Lambda syntax is derived from the functional interface, represents inputs and body including exceptions similar to a normal method declaration. The expression is formed as : (input) → {body}

Consider the following code segment, a copy of the same example as above.

21

```
// DissectingLambda.java

// Return is implicit as the body is no more a simple
statement/expression

t -> {
  return t.isCancelledTrade();
}
```

For multi-line code (each line is separated by a semi-colon delimiter) body, we need to use curly braces with an explicit return. For example, look at an other example where lambda's body is enclosed (simple logic) within braces where the return is mandatory:

```
// GreetingExample.java

// explicit return type required when braces are used
Greeting greetingLambda = s ->{
  return "Hello, " +s;
};
```

Lambda Type

Now that we have covered the syntax basics, next step is to find the mechanism of how a lambda is formed. The formation of a lambda expression, as mentioned earlier, depends on the definition of the functional interface.

Let's consider a simple example of Hello, World! A functional interface (interface with one abstract method) for the greeting message is defined like this:

```
// GreetingExample.java

// Functional interface
interface Greeting {
  String sayHello(String name);
}
```

This interface has a single abstract method sayHello, which accepts a name (String) and returns a message (String). As it has a single abstract method, we can define a lambda expression with Greeting as its type.

The sayHello method accepts an input of type String. Our lambda's left part should resemble this. Hence the left hand side of lambda can be written as:

```
// Left part of the lambda
(String msg)
```

The right hand side of the lambda is the logic applied on the given input. The logic is to print out a message to the console. The code segment shown below shows this:

```
// Right part of the lambda
System.out.println("Hello, "+msg);
```

Now that we have the left and right part of the lambda, both parts are put together with an arrow operator operator separating them, thus producing a lambda expression:

```
// Final lambda expression
(String msg) -> System.out.println("Hello, "+msg);
```

Let's compare this with the concrete implementation of the Greeting interface. If were to implement this class, we will have a concrete implementation of the sayHello method will be somewhere along the lines as shown below:

```
Greeting oldGreeting = new Greeting(){
  @Override
  public void sayHello(String msg) {
    System.out.println("Hello, "+msg);
  }
};

// This is the transformation to a lambda!
(String msg) -> System.out.println("Hello, "+msg);
```

Comparing the traditional implementation of Greeting interface with the lambda expression, you can see how the highlighted code from the traditional class implementation made it into a lambda! The main differences are the name of the method is foregone as well as the rest of the boiler plate code, leaving us with a simple expression.

Lastly, if we need to assign this expression to a variable, we should assign to our functional interface, from which we derived our lambda in the first place:

```
//Type is a functional interface
Greeting greetingLambda =
  (String msg) -> System.out.println("Hello, "+msg);
```

TradeMerger Lambda Example

To cement out understanding of formation of a lambda expression, let's consider another example, this time with two inputs and returning an object.

For this purpose, we create an interface called Merger which defines a contract for merging two trades producing a brand new trade. We define a single abstract method named merge accepting two trades:

```
// TradeMerger.java

// A functional interface for merging the trades

interface Merger{
  Trade merge(Trade t1, Trade t2);
}
```

As the method accepts two inputs, we write the input parameters in the parenthesis on the left hand side of the expression. On the right hand side we merge these two input trades to returning a merged trade (business logic is omitted for brevity). This is shown in the code segment below:

```
// TradeMerger.java

// Lambda expression
(Trade t1, Trade t2) -> {
  Trade mergedTrade = new Trade();
  ....
  return mergedTrade;
}

// Even better, drop the type declarations
(t1, t2) -> {
  Trade mergedTrade = new Trade();
  ....
  return mergedTrade;
}
```

If you wish, you can drop the types of input arguments (as shown in the second part of the example snippet above) as they can be inferred by the compiler.

The last piece in the puzzle is the type of this lambda. The functional interface itself becomes the type of the lambda expression. Hence, the above lambda expression is assigned to a functional interface `Merger` as shown below:

The type of a lambda is a Functional Interface. A functional interface is a normal interface with one feature: it must have a single abstract method if it expected to represent a lambda.

```
// TradeMerger.java

// The lambda is assigned to a functional interface
Merger mergedTrade  = (t1, t2) -> {
   ....
   return mergedTrade;
}
```

Let's wrap up here and jump to next chapter to work with more concepts of lambdas.

Summary

In this chapter, we laid the foundations of creating and forming a lambda expression. We learned that a lambda resembles a method signature, however syntax should adhere to a special format. We looked at lambda examples, along with creating custom functional interfaces and respective lambdas.

5. WORKING WITH LAMBDAS

By now, we have gathered good understanding of lambdas, albeit from a high level. It is time to start diving into deep to understand important concepts such as target typing, scoping, inheritance and others.

Target Typing

We learned earlier that the type of a lambda expression is a functional interface. We also know since Java is a strongly typed language, it is mandatory to declare types else the compiler will moan.

Target typing can be understood in the context in which the lambda expression is being used. There are two categories of contexts that we can work with when types are concerned: an *assignment* context and an *invocation* context. In both cases, the compiler is clever enough to infer the type of a lambda expression.

Assignment Context

We have a luxury of creating a lambda expression and passing it to a method without having to worry about assigning it it a local variable. However, there are times we may need to create variables referring lambda expressions. For example, in the following snippet, we have an expression assigned to a `Merger` type:

```
// TradeMerger.java

// The lambda is assigned to a functional interface
Merger mergedTrade  = (t1, t2) -> {
    ....
    return mergedTrade;
}
```

We have assigned the lambda expression to a variable so it can be referenced elsewhere in the program. Here, in this example, we are declaring the type of the expression explicitly (assigned to Merger) and by doing so, the compiler can infer the types of the input parameters should we not declare them in the definition of the lambda expression. That is, in the above example, you can see that we omitted the types of input arguments t1 and t2.

In order to find the type of these input arguments, the compiler uses the *assignment* context to derive them. It will have to perform few steps during this target typing process, listed here below:

The compiler first looks at the variable type (Merger in this case) and reads the method signature of that interface (Merger has one method merger). The signature of the Merger's merge method indicates that it accepts two inputs, both of Trade type which means our lambda expression's input arguments must of of the same type (Trade) too. The compiler applies such logic and infers that the t1 and t2 are of type Trade.

In earlier examples, we have seen a case where the type of the input arguments being omitted. See the following lambda expression, passed into to a method, which prints out the greeting:

```
// The type of msg parameter is dropped!
msg -> System.out.println(msg);
```

The type of the input parameter, msg, in this case is not declared explicitly. How does the compiler know that it's of a certain type? Well, this is inferred from the assignment context, too. As the type of the above expression is a Greeting, the method it has accepts a String as input and returns void. And this input should match to that of the lambda's input - hence the msg is of type String. Similarly, the compiler inspects the return value of the method, void, in this case. The compiler checks if the lambda expression is returning a void too, which it does. So far all seems to be in order. Last thing is to find out if the method throws any exceptions. Our method here doesn't throw any exceptions, hence this check will not be performed.

In the case of a lambda expression assigned to a variable, the context is the *type* to which the lambda is assigned to. The compiler derives the type by matching against the functional interface.

As all the checks are performed successfully, the compiler is satisfied with the target type that we've assigned to the lambda and no errors or warnings pop up.

Invocation Context

When we create a lambda expression inline, the compiler takes the help of the invocation context to resolve the type of the expression. Suppose we have a method that accepts a functional interface, `Runnable`, as its input argument, like shown here:

```
public void runMe(Runnable r){
   new Thread(r).start();
}
```

We know that a lambda expression can be developed with a `Runnable` as its type. Hence, we can invoke the `runMe` method by passing a lambda expression as its input argument inline. See the code snippet below:

```
public void runMe(( ) -> {
   sendEmail();
   notifyAccounts();
});
```

We are not creating an instance of a `Runnable` here, instead we are passing a block of code to a method (code as data) which is a powerful feature. We are setting the lambda expression on the `runMe` method on the fly.

How does the compiler know that the given lambda expression fits the bill? Well, the same target typing theory we learned for assignment context applies here too. The `runMe` method accepts a `Runnable` as the input argument, so our lambda expression *must be of* a `Runnable` type. The compiler goes through the usual checks that we have seen earlier. The take away point is that target typing enables the type of the lambda expression to be inferred from the context where it is being executed.

Lambda Scoping

Like other programming languages, Java language too has scoping rules for objects, classes, methods and variables. As a developer, we are expected to learn about class, inner class and method level scopes without fail. Once we become familiar with the language, these scopes gets ingrained onto our mind. The lambda expressions, as they are code blocks, have some rules of scoping too.

Lexical Scope

A lambda expression scope does not extend beyond the method in which it is created. It is lexically scoped, meaning it exhibits same scope as of the enclosed method. This is termed as *lexical scoping*.

Whatever the rules and policies apply to methods, the same applies to lambda expressions created in the host method too. The use of `this` or `super`, including the access of static types, is same for both methods and lambdas.

> Lambda is lexically scoped, meaning the scope of a lambda expression is same as that of its enclosing method.

Consider the following example:

```java
// LambdaThisStaticSuperAccess.java

//Class demonstrating the lexical scoping functionality

class LambdaThisStaticSuperAccess extends SuperScope{
   private String instanceName="instanceVariableName";
   private static String staticName = "staticVariableName";

   Runnable runnableLambda = () ->{
     print("Super variable: "+super.superVariable);
     print("Instance variable: "+this.instanceName);
     print("Static variable: "
           +LambdaThisStaticSuperAccess.staticName);
   };
}
// Super class
public class SuperScope {
   String superName = "superVariableName";
}
```

Here, we defined a class `LambdaThisStaticSuperAccess` which has two variables, an instance variable (`instanceName`) as well as a static variable (`staticName`). It extends a super class called `SuperScope`, which declares its own variable (`superName`). In our lambda expression (runnableLambda), we are accessing these variables as we would do from a normal method using `this`, `super` or class name for static type.

The output is shown below when you execute the above program:

```
// Output from LambdaThisStaticSuperAccess.java

Super variable: superVariableName
Instance variable: instanceVariableName
Static variable: staticVariableName
```

Accessing *this* in an Anonymous class

However, accessing the this in an anonymous class differs to that of a lambda. The anonymous class takes the scope of the class that creates it, while the lambda takes the scope of an enclosing class where it was declared.

Let's check this out by creating an anonymous Runnable implementation which accesses hashCode method as well as a Runnable lambda doing the same thing. Both printout the hash code of the class they were created from, when executed.

```
// LambdaAnonymousScope.java

// Outputting Hashcode from a lambda
new Thread(()->print("Lambda hashcode:"+this.hashCode()))
  .start();

// Outputting Hashcode from an anonymous class
new Thread(new Runnable(){
  @Override
  public void run() {
    print("Anonymous hashcode:"+this.hashCode());
  }
}).start();

// Output
Lambda hashcode:1159190947
Anonymous hashcode:557931705
```

The anonymous class's this.hashCode invocation is fetching the Runnable instance's hash code - thus, the anonymous class's scope is enclosed with the class that it is created. The lambda's this.hashCode is using the LambdaAnonymousScope instance, the class in which the lambda was defined (thus the lambda's scope is of the enclosing class, just like a method).

Redeclaring the Variable

Variables are not to be re-declared in a lambda expression. That is, if a variable has already been declared elsewhere in the class, we cannot reassign or re-declare it in a lambda.

In the following code, note that a local variable myName is declared in the method, but we try to declare the same variable in the lambda expression too:

```
//LambdaRedeclaringVariables.java

private void testLocalVariable() {
   final String myName = "Modified Name";;
   IComponent cc = () -> {
     // Error! Redeclaring the variable is illegal
     // String myName = null; // Uncomment
     return myName;
   };
}
```

This is like having two variables with the same name in a code block, which is illegal and hence the compiler will not be happy. The takeaway point is that scoping rules of a method apply to a lambda too.

Capturing Lambdas

So far we have developed lambda expressions that uses its own input parameters. For example, in the Greeting lambda shown below, msg is the input argument and the body prints out the msg to the console:

```
// CapturingLambda.java

Greeting greetingLambda =
   msg -> System.out.println("Hello, "+msg);
```

We say the msg is a lambda variable and its scope is restricted to the lambda expression only. The compiler will be unhappy if we try to access the msg variable anywhere else other than the lambda expression, even in the method in which the lambda was created.

Consider the following code example:

```
// CapturingLambda.java

private void accessLambdaVariables() {
  Greeting g = (name) -> {
    print(defaultGreeting + name);
  };
  // Cannot access the lambda's input variable
  // print("Can I access lambda's variable:"+name);
}
```

When we access the lambda's input variable name outside the lambda expression, the compiler complains that the name cannot be resolved. Hence, the scope of the variables declared as lambda parameters or used inside lambda are not visible to outside world.

But the opposite is fine, i.e, lambdas accessing class's instance or static variables is legal. These are the variables that are not passed to lambdas, but created elsewhere in the enclosing method or the class.

Consider the following example where an instance variable (defaultGreeting) has been accessed in the lambda expression:

```
// CapturingLambda.java
public class CapturingLambda {
  // instance variable
  private String defaultGreeting = "Howdy, ";

  private void accessInstanceVariables() {
    // Lambda expression accessing the instance variable
    Greeting g = (name) -> {
      // Accessing an instance variable is allowed
      print(defaultGreeting + name);
    };
}
```

The lambda expression is accessing the defaultGreeting variable with no scoping issues to resolve. There is a name for such variable - a *free variable*. Any variable that's not been declared as the parameter of the lambda expression but is accessed from the surrounding scope is called a free variable. The instance variables or static variables along with local variables fall into this category.

A capturing lambda captures (copies) the variables declared elsewhere in the class.

The lambda that uses these free variables is called a *capturing lambda*. That is, lambda *captures* (or copies) the any input arguments given to it, in the sense the values of these input variables are copied.

A word of advice on the use of free variables in lambda expressions. Although it is legal to access class's variables from a lambda, doing so may result in side effects. Side-effect is an unwished modification of state in a program. In a purely functional programming style, shared state is not undertaken and the side-effect-free functions are advised.

Local Variables (Effectively Final State)

In Java 7 and earlier, in an anonymous class, we can capture local variables as long as the local variables are declared as `final`. This rule has been relaxed in Java 8. The lambda expressions, on the other hand can access the local variables provided on one condition - the variables are never mutated. The local variables must be *effectively final* when accessed, though they need not be declared as `final` explicitly.

It is *optional* to declare the local variables `final` but the expectation is that they are not modified in the code, effectively making them final

Consider the following example:

```
// EffectivelyFinalLambda.java

private void execute() {
  // Local non-final variable
  int count = 0;
  // Lambda expression which modifies the count
  // Count is a local variable, must be effectively final
  // Lambda doesn't compile
  new Thread(() -> print(count++) ).start();
}
```

We declared a local variable `count` which gets incremented in the lambda expression. Changing the value of a captured variable (`count`) inside a lambda expression accounts to an an error (shown below) saying that our variable violated the *effectively final* scope restriction:

```
// Compilation error when local variables
// are modified in a lambda:

Local variable count defined in an enclosing scope must be
final or effectively final
```

Hence, keep in mind that the local variables are treated as immutable objects or assigned only once.

Why Effectively Final?

There is a valid reason behind having the effectively final modifier restriction on the method scoped variables.

We know that the local variables exists on stack memory as oppose to heap memory for class or instance variables. Any data on the stack memory cannot be shared by any other thread (thus no issue of thread safety). No other thread can have access to that stack apart from itself, the original thread.

However, there may be a situation where a lambda may still be running although the Thread that's created it may have been recycled and long gone. If the values were erased too, then the long running lambda expression will encounter errors. To avoid this situation, the lambda expression is required to capture the values of these local variables expecting no modifications to the data.

Avoid using variables declared outside the lambda expression. A good programming practice is to treat the lambda as a black box, thus passing the data to the expression on every invocation.

Modifying Class/Instance Variables

The restriction of modifying the local variables of a method scope does not apply to other variable like class or instance variables. We are free to override the class/instance variables in our lambda without any issues. Consider the following code segment:

```
// EffectivelyFinalLambda.java

public class EffectivelyFinalLambda {
  // Instance variable
  private String instanceVariable = "Instance Variable";
  private void modifyClassInstanceVariable() {
   // Local non-final variable
   instanceVariable = "Modified Instance Variable";
   new Thread(() -> print(instanceVariable) ).start();
  }
}
// Output:
Modified Instance Variable
```

As you can observe, the instanceVariable is an instance variable declared with an initial value. However, we are resetting the instanceVariable again in a lambda expression defined in a method. This is perfectly legal, although it may seem violation of the effectively final rule.

Unfortunately the effectively final rule doesn't apply when class or instance variables are modified. It is not enforced by the compiler or by the runtime. The compiler will not be providing us with any hints, warnings or errors, its solely up to us to be aware of. We should be really careful not to violate this rule as it might lead to serious thread safety issues.

My advise would be to follow the path of the local variables (effectively final) for class and instance variables too. This way, we can avoid plethora of subtle but detrimental thread safety issues as well as avoiding any likelihood of concurrency bugs surfacing up which are hard to catch and debug.

Type Inference

In our earlier examples of lambdas, we worked with them where the type of the input parameters were omitted. We briefly learned about how the compiler uses assignment context to derive those types. The process of deducing the types is called *Type Inference*. For example, in the following snippet below, the type of the input parameter t is omitted:

```
// Input parameter type is ignored
Tradable tradableLambda = ( t ) -> check(t);
```

The compiler is clever enough to infer the type by evaluating the context in which the lambda is operating. In the above example, compiler uses the assignment context to figure out that Tradable interface's single method check takes in a parameter of type Trade.

Type inference is not new to Java 8, you may have worked with it without noticing. For example, here in this example, we declare a HashMap with an integer as key and String as value as well as the same declaration by omitting the types:

```
// Explicit declaration of types
Map<Integer, String> map = new HashMap<Integer, String>();

// Types are inferred from the context
Map<Integer, String> map = new HashMap<>();
```

The type parameters will be identified by the context (the Map is declared with Integer and String parameters) in which it is being executed. It's not only un-clutters the code, easy to read as well.

How does the compiler inference system work?

Remember, the type of a lambda expression is a functional interface? We know that lambdas can be assigned to a variable of functional interface implementations or any method that takes in a functional interface as its parameter.

The Java compiler knows that target type of this lambda expression as a functional interface and accordingly it evaluates the types based on the condition that the input parameters of the lambda must match to the method input parameters. Stating the types is optional and we don't need to explicit declare the types unless there's a conflict or confusion.

Summary

In this chapter, we looked at some of the advanced topics on lambdas. We explored target typing and lambda scoping in detail. We also worked on capturing lambdas. We discussed the rationalisation behind effectively final clause and finally understood the concept of type interface.

5. ADVANCED LAMBDAS

When working with lambdas, we may have to invoke call business logic defined elsewhere in a method or a separate class. Lambdas allow accessing other methods and constructors by a way of referencing them. The process is called method or constructor referencing. In this chapter, we will learn about method and constructor references.

Method References

Often we may wish to refer to an existing method in our lambda expression. This method may have been declared elsewhere in the other classes or packages, like in a common module or may be in a third party library. Java 8 introduced a concept of referencing to the exiting method from a lambda expression - this is called *method referencing*.

Consider the following utility method defined in a `References` class where we check if a given movie is an all-time classic:

```
// References.java

public class References {
   ....
   // An ordinary method to check if the movie is a classic
   public boolean isClassic(int movieId) {
    return ( movieId < 1000 );
   }
}
```

As this is a public method, it is expected to be used by other clients including lambda expressions too. If we need to find a classic movie from a lambda expression, you can simply invoke the method from the lambda, just the way you would normally do to invoke a method:

```
// References.java

public class References {
...

// Lambda calling a method defined elsewhere in the class.
MovieChecker isClassic = movieId -> isClassic(movieId);

// method defined in the class
public boolean isClassic(int movieId) {
..
}
```

As you can see, the isClassic method is referred from the lambda without a second thought. We can also call the methods from a lambda defined in a separate class or a library too. For example, say a ReferenceUtil class defines a isClassic method too, which we would like to refer to from our lambda defined in References class. All we do is to create an instance of the ReferenceUtil and invoke the method on it, same as what we do in Java to invoke a method:

```
// References.java

// Create an instance of the other class
ReferenceUtil util = new ReferenceUtil();

// and invoke the method via the instance in our lambda
MovieChecker isClassic = movieId->util.isClassic(movieId);
```

Our lambda expression is not doing much other than delegating the call to the ReferenceUtil instance. However, we can condense this expression even further to shorten the lambda expression using the *method referencing* functionality.

Method references are shorthand for lambda expressions, referencing to an existing method.

Method references are a shorthand to lambda expressions - an easy expressive way of delegating the call to an existing method. The above lambda expression can be written as:

```
// References.java#instanceMethodRef

// Lambda with a method reference
MovieChecker isClassicLambda = util::isClassic;
```

Pay particular attention to the right hand side of the assignment, the lambda body. The lambda uses a special operator (::) to refer to the isClassic method that already exists in the util object. The double colon (::) is an indication that we are using the method reference functionality. The part to the left of the colon is the host class of the method to be invoked, references in this case. While the right part after the colon is the name of the method itself, isClassic in this case.

There are few peculiarities about this method reference syntax, if you observe carefully. We don't represent input and body delimited by an arrow token anymore (as we do for expressing a lambda expression). When wiring up the method name, the parenthesis is not required (the isClassic doesn't have a parenthesis). Also, any mention of input parameters is ignored too.

The reason for not providing the parenthesis and method parameters is actually simple: we are simply declaring a *reference* to an existing method but not invoking the method at all (and hence called method referencing!). So, when you are working with method referencing, make sure you drop the lambda syntax and pick up the referencing syntax carefully.

Check out one more example of lambda expression using a method reference.

```
// References.java#exampleMethodReferences

// A lambda calling an existing method (greet)
Greeting greetingLambdaReference = s -> {
  return greet(s);
};

// A lambda calling existing method, using method ref
Greeting greetingLambdaReference = this::greet;
```

The this variable refers to the instance which provides the greet method. Do note that there are no more input parameters or arrow tokens.

Static Method References

Let's see another case where we have a static method (shown below) isHorror defined in ReferenceUtil class that we wish to refer from a

```
```

lambda expression in `References` class:

```
// ReferenceUtil.java#isHorror

// A utility method to check horror movie
public static boolean isHorror(int movieId) {
    return (movieId >10000 && movieId < 20000);
}
```

Let's first look at a way of using this method from our lambda expression. This is shown in the code example below:

```
// References.java#staticMethodRef

// Invoking a static method normally (no method ref)

MovieChecker isClassic = movieId ->
    ReferenceUtil.isHorror(movieId);
```

The lambda expression is simply invoking the static method on the util class, as expected. There's no surprise here. However, we can take advantage of method referencing to make this lambda concise:

```
// References.java#staticMethodRef

// Static method reference usage
MovieChecker isClassicLambda = ReferenceUtil::isHorror;
```

The method parameters and parenthesis are not required in this case too.

Arbitrary Type Method References

Lastly, if we wish to invoke a method of any arbitrary type, say a method `isBoxOfficeHit` defined in a `ArbitraryClass` class, we can use the same principe of method references to invoke the method:

```
// References.java#arbitraryMethodRef

private void arbitraryMethodRef() {
  // Lambda version using class reference
  MovieChecker boHit = ArbitraryClass::isBoxOfficeHit;
}

// An arbitrary class with BO hit method
class ArbitraryClass{
  public static boolean isBoxOfficeHit(int movieId) {
    // Logic in finding the box office collections here.
    return true;
  }
}
```

Here, the `ArbitraryClass` is a class declared else where and our lambda is invoking its method using method reference shorthand.

Constructor References

Similar to methods, constructors can also be referenced from a lambda expression with an easy-to-read syntax. The main difference between constructor and method references is that the method name is always `new` in a constructor reference.

For example, `ArrayList::new` indicates the simple constructor reference for creating a new array list. When it comes to the constructor referencing, there's one tricky part: remember a class can have multiple constructors with varied list of parameters? Also remember, referencing mechanism ignores the parameters, right? There is a bit of explanation needed in order to understand this mechanism as it is important you understand the referencing for various constructors thoroughly.

Say we have an `Employee` class with a two constructors - one that creates an `Employee` by taking an `id` while other creates the `Employee` by taking `id` and `name`. We define the class here:

```
// Employee.java

// Employee class with two constructors
class Employee {
  ....
  public Employee(int id) {
    // Logic for creating an employee with an id
    ...
  }
  public Employee(int id, String name){
    // Logic for creating an employee with an id and name.
    ...
  }
}
```

In order to reference these constructors, we design two functional interfaces, each defining the above constructors individually. Consider the following interface definitions:

```
// Employee.java

// Interface representing the first constructor
interface EmployeeById {
  public Employee create(int id);
}

// Interface representing the second constructor
interface EmployeeByName {
  public Employee create(int id, String employee);
}
```

Keep a note that we must create *individual functional interface for each of the constructors defined in the class* (of course, only for those constructors that we would wish to use constructor references when defining lambda expressions).

Using our knowledge so far, we can create a lambda expression for each of the above functional interfaces in our usual way without using constructor references:

```
// Employee.java

// Lambda invoking the first constructor - no const refs
EmployeeById empLambda = id -> new Employee(id);

// Lambda invoking the second constructor - no const refs
EmployeeByName empNameLambda =
   (id, name) -> new Employee(id, name);
```

However, we can use the constructor references to shorten them. The two lambda expressions using the references to constructors can be defined as shown in the following snippet:

```
// Employee.java
// Both have the same constructor reference

// Constructor reference invocation for first constructor
EmployeeById empLambdaConstRef = Employee::new;

// Constructor reference invocation for second constructor
EmployeeByName empNameLambdaConstRef = Employee::new;
```

Did you notice the oddity of the constructor reference declaration in the above snippet? Both of them have *exact declaration of the reference* (Employee::new). How does the compiler know to select a particular constructor?

Well, again, that depends on the context in which the lambda expression is defined. Let's see how does the context help choose the right constructor. Notice that the type of the first lambda expression defined as (the context is assignment context):

```
// Note the type of the lambda assigned to.
EmployeeById empLambdaConstRef = Employee::new;
```

The assignment context dictates that the lambda that's been declared is EmployeeById. We know that EmployeeById has an abstract method create that accepts an id returning an Employee. The lambda

Constructor references are shorthand names to a lambda expression invoking constructors. The method name will always be written as new.

expression gets created assigning to a type EmployeeById. However, the lambda expression can be replaced with the constructor reference and

43

hence `Employee::new` should be the shorthand to `id -> new Employee(id)` which represents `EmployeeById` functional interface which in turn is the constructor with id as its parameter.

```
// Employee.java
// Interface representing the first constructor
interface EmployeeById {
  public Employee create(int id);
}

// Lambda invoking the first constructor - no const refs
EmployeeById empLambda = id -> new Employee(id);

// Using constructor reference
EmployeeById empLambdaConstRef = Employee::new;
```

Hence, the constructor reference is resolved to the first constructor taking a id as input.

Following the same principle, the second lambda's context is `EmployeeByName` interface, hence it must be the constructor with two inputs - an `id` and `name` although the constructor reference points the same reference `Employee::new`.

The name of the method in your interface can be any name, doesn't need to be `create` as I had them defined above.

Array Constructor References

There's another case of creating constructor references for arrays? For example, if we have arrays of different types, how do we create a lambda expression referring to the appropriate constructor? In this case, we use `ClassName::new` syntax. Let's follow through using an example.

For producing an array of `Strings`, say we have designed an interface called `StringArray` which creates an array of `Strings` given a size as its input parameter.

```
// ArrayReferences.java

//Interface creating an array of Strings
interface StringArray{
  String[] create(int size);
}

// Lambda without references
StringArray sArrayLambda = (size) -> new String[size];
```

However, we are lazy and don't want to write the full lambda expression. Here's where constructor references comes handy:

```
// ArrayReferences.java

StringArray sArrayLambdaMethodRef = String[]::new;
```

We simply used the class name (String[]) to deduce the method reference feature in case of arrays. Similarly, if we are working for a custom domain array, like array of Trades, here's what we need to do:

```
interface TradeArray{
  Trade[] create(int size);
}

// Lambda using array references
TradeArray tradesLambdaMethodRef = Trade[]::new;
```

Summary

In this chapter, we learned about implementing the lambda expressions using method and constructor references. We understood that these references are simply shorthands referring to actual methods and constructors. We also looked at the assignment context which is used to deduce the reference to an actual method by a lambda expression.

6. INTERFACES

Prior to Java 8, once an interface was written, it is more or less written in stone. If changes were made to an interface, the whole process of recompiling, reengineering, retesting and regression of the codebase was necessary. It is quite unproductive and inefficient.

We know how important is backward compatibility in Java world. Java excelled and exceeded expectations in the area of source and binary compatibility compared to its peers. This has been a great strength but at the same time caused a great pain too. Fortunately, the pain is eased by changing the course by overhauling interfaces in Java 8. The interface definitions are really spiced up. In this chapter, we run through the changes brought in by Java 8 related to interfaces in detail.

Backward Compatibility

As we all know, the interface is the mother of any user library. Designers start building frameworks or libraries starting with a simple interface, weaving it with others and building the system as they go along. If we wish to modify an existing interface by adding a new method or changing the signature of an existing method, it would automatically fail with the earlier versioned compilers.

Most of our libraries were designed a while back and some existed since Java's early days. Nonetheless, modifications to these libraries are inevitable as more and more features and functionalities are long overdue. These features however impose structural modifications to the libraries and without sacrificing the backward compatibility, there's no efficient way to accommodate the changes. The inflexibility of an interface posed a great headache to Java designers.

While Java 8 is embracing functional programming style and introducing lambda expressions. It would be a real shame if the existing libraries can't be upgraded to use the lambdas.

Fortunately, Java designers took a brave and clever decision - to overhaul the interfaces and unlocking them to realise their full potential. Going forward, we can change the interface definition without having to worry about the compilation errors. We add new methods or modify existing methods with no complains from the compiler. In my opinion, modernising the interface is one of the best achievements of Java 8.

Interface Unlocking

So, what have the Java Designers done to our good old interface?

In Java 8, we can update an existing interface to modify the method declarations. Modifying the interface will not be causing any more of the compiler issues. In addition to this, we can add *concrete* method implementations to an interface. The mighty interface can have a full blown method implementations similar to abstract classes. The methods defined and declared in an interface with full implementation fall into two categories: *default* and *static* methods.

Another big stride is the introduction of the functional interface. As we learned in earlier chapters, a functional interface is a crucial step to leap into a functional programming world. It is used as a target type for a lambda expression. Of course a functional interface's only restriction is that it can't have more than one abstract method declared if it is intended for being the target type of a lambda. In addition to these changes around interface structure, theres's also an *intersection type* introduced in Java 8, which is discussed in this chapter.

Functional Interfaces

A functional interface and a lambda expression go hand in hand, they are married for life. We briefly touched upon the type of a lambda expression in earlier chapters. To recap, the type of a lambda expression is a functional interface. A lambda can be passed to a method that expects a functional interface.

A functional interface is *a special interface with one and only one abstract method*. Functional interfaces are fundamental to lambdas and functional programming.

As Java is a strongly typed language, it is mandatory to declare the type of a variable being used in the class, else the compiler will moan dutifully. Fortunately, to represent a lambda expression, Java designers chose a strategy of re-using the existing anonymous classes in the form of functional interfaces. But what is a functional interface? Why is it important when creating lambdas?

Consider the following interface definition for admitting a Patient:

```
// Interfaces.java

// Hospital admitting patients
interface Hospital{
    void admit(Patient patient);
}
```

Here, we have a single method admit accepting a Patient. Behaviour of the method can be implemented by any lambda expression so long the interface sticks to the contract of providing one and only one abstract method. Look at the example lambdas here below:

```
// Interfaces.java

// Lambda expressions
Hospital emergencyAddmittance =
  (p)->print("Admitting patient to A&E: "+p);

Hospital generalAdmittance = (p) -> {
  print("Admitting patient to a general ward: "+p);
  // calling an existing method
  general(p);
};

// Or we could shorten the lambda using the method ref
Hospital generalAdmittanceMethodRef = this::general;
```

Having said that, we can have an interface with one abstract method but still don't use it as a functional interface. For example, the following is a Factory interface for creating Vehicle objects:

```
// Interfaces.java

// An interface that may or may be not used for lambda
interface Factory {
  Vehicle create(int id);
}
```

The users of the library will always use this interface for creating a specific vehicle, a car,van or a bus in a traditional way (non-lambda specific implementations) by implementing it. But, there's nothing stopping us to create a lambda expression out of it, as shown here:

```
// Interfaces.java

// Lambda expression for the above factory
Factory factory = id -> new Vehicle(id);
```

If we start using this interface as a functional interface and accordingly expect lambdas popping out of it, we need make sure our intention is documented via Javadoc or some other means (or using annotation @FunctionalInterface which we will see in our next section). If the intention is not clearly stated, the functionality can be broken when a team member adds an extra method to that interface, like we did here:

```
// Not a functional interface anymore!
interface Factory{
   Vehicle create(int id);

   // Additional abstract method
   boolean scrap(int id);
}
```

Adding the additional abstract method scrap to the interface breaks the contract of a functional interface-lambda expression. All our lambda expressions will be invalidated and we will have a field day fixing the issues. Its no fault of your colleague as you didn't document your intent. Let's see how we can fix this issue without having to work very hard!

@FunctionalInterface Annotation

We can decorate a functional interface with the @FunctionalInteface annotation to fulfil the functional interface-lambda contract. This is a new annotation introduced in Java 8, which acts as a safety guard avoiding the inadvertent use of the interface. Annotating the interface is nothing but formalising the functional interface contract.

Let's decorate the Factory interface with this annotation as shown below:

```
@FunctionalInteface
interface Factory{
  Vehicle create(int id);
  ....
}
```

Adding any additional abstract methods to the annotated interface will create compile time errors, thus abiding to the contract. Note that the annotation is purely *optional*. Annotating will help development IDEs to identify the contract and report issues if the contract breaks at compile time. Though it is optional, I highly recommend the use of the aforementioned tag to let out intention of a functional interfaces known to the world.

In addition to having one abstract method, it can also have many number of concrete methods (`static` and `default` methods) and still maintain its functional interface status. The compiler will be happy as long as you keep your end of the bargain of maintaining a lone abstract method definition in the interface.

Default and Static Methods

We all know adding any form of concrete implementations to an interface prior to Java 8 was impossible and moreover illegal. However this has changed beginning with Java 8. Going forward, we can add concrete implementations to an interface. The interface allows us to fully define and implement methods. However, all the concrete methods must be declared either as a `default` or a `static` method.

The concrete implementations belonging to an instance of an implementation class are called as `default` methods while those associated to a class are called `static` methods. Let's explore them in detail.

Default Methods

Default methods are the concrete code bodies defined in the interface prefixed with a special keyword `default`. Look at the following snippet, where we have defined a fully implemented `default` methods:

```java
// Diner.java
@FunctionalInterface
public interface Diner {
  // abstract method
  String order(String order);

  // default methods
  default String getCoffee() {
    return "Cappuccino";
  }
  default String getEnglishBreakfast() {
    return "Bacon,Sausage,Eggs,Mushrooms,Beans and Toast";
  }

  default String getIndianBreakfast() {
    return "Idly, Sambar and a Dosa";
  }
}
```

Previously, in order to provide default implementations, the usual strategy we used was to create an abstract class and implement the required implementation in it. However, beginning with Java 8, we can certainly take advantage of default methods to provide concrete implementations in the interface itself rather than creating an abstract class.

The only requirement for making a method default is to prefix it with the default keyword

default *method inheritance*

Any class that extends the interface automatically inherits the default methods declared in that interface. For instance, the following snippet shows inheriting order method from the super interface Diner:

```java
// DinerImpl.java

public class DinerImpl implements Diner{
  @Override
  public String order(String order) {
    StringBuilder breakfastOrder = new StringBuilder();
    // Accessing interface's default methods
    String coffee = getCoffee();
    String breakfast = getEnglishBreakfast();

    return breakfastCoffee
        .append(coffee).append(" with ")
        .append(breakfast).toString();
  }
}
```

We can also create a lambda expression for the abstract method `order` defined in the `Diner` functional interface. Look at the code sample that uses a lambda to create a breakfast order:

```
// DinerImpl.java
public class DinerImpl implements Diner{
  // method that accepts a lambda
  public String order(String order, Diner lambda) {
    return lambda.order(order);
  }

  public static void main(String[] args) {
    DinerImpl impl = new DinerImpl();

    // Lambda expression
    Diner dineOrder = s -> {
      return "Breakfast on its way for "+s;
    };
    // send the order and lambda!
    String lambdaOrder=impl.order("Mr Harry", dineOrder);
  }
}
```

Static Methods

Similar to `default` methods, you can add concrete `static` methods to an interface. The only difference is that static methods belong to class and not to the instance. Let us enhance the `Diner` interface with a `static` method that accepts a bill payment. The code is shown below:

```
@FunctionalInterface
public interface Diner {
  ....
  static String payBill(double billAmount) {
    return "Ciao, see you next time!";
  }
}
```

So, prefixing a `static` keyword in front of the method makes it a `static` interface method. We use the `Class` name to access the static method, as shown in the following snippet

```
//Accessing the static method
Diner.payBill(5.60);
```

Both `static` and `default` methods are quite handy when we wish to provide some functionality at an interface level which can be inherited to sub-classes.

Interfaces Vs Abstract Classes

In Java, we are very familiar with abstract class strategy. If we need to provide some partial implementation of a design or perhaps default behaviour, we normally follow a abstract class strategy. We provide an abstract class with some methods fully defined while leaving others to be implemented by its subclass.

In Java 8, interfaces can take this job too. They can consist of concrete methods which are full blown implementations of a functionality similar to a concrete method defined in an abstract class. Here, we compare and contrast both strategies.

Common Functionality

If our requirement is to share a common functionality within a set of related classes, perhaps abstract class strategy is the best. If you would like your subclasses to inherit state in addition to behaviour, then they should extend the abstract class. We also have a free hand in declaring the access modifiers on fields and methods - that is - we can have `public` or `private` or `static` or non-final methods and fields according to our class design.

But if our intention is to provide behaviour derived from multiple types, we should use interface strategy. We can implement as many interfaces as we wish depending on the type of behaviour we would like to derive. Sometimes, if we wish to merge various functionalities or derive from different set of interfaces, then this strategy is advised. Remember, we are inheriting the behaviour using interface's default method mechanism.

Instantiation

Abstract classes and interfaces have one thing in common - they cannot be instantiated. Any behaviour we define in them can only be inherited or derived via other classes. Their sole purpose is to be used by other classes., hence they are very good candidates for implementing common behaviour patterns.

Fields and Methods

There's a potential difference in the way the fields and methods are structured and accessed in an abstract class versus an interface. Abstract classes may have instance fields of any type (such as `public`, `private`, `final`, `static` etc). This is in contrast to what interface fields can be: `public`, `static` and `final` implicitly. The new default methods which were earlier implemented in abstract classes have now paved their way into interfaces which can only be given `public` access due to the nature of the interface contract.

So don't feel obligated to use or not to use abstract classes or interfaces. For me, if state is to be inherited, I will stick to an abstract class while if reusing behaviour is the priority then I will go with the interface strategy.

Inheriting Behaviour

When it comes to inheritance, the Java language follows certain set of rules. A class can extend a single class, but can implement multiple interfaces. Because interfaces in Java 8 can have concrete method implementations, our classes can extend various interfaces drawing in the multiple inheritance functionality which was otherwise impossible in previous versions. We can use this multiple inheritance feature to reuse code effectively, especially when designing frameworks and libraries.

For example, we have a method `make` in `Engine` interface and also `model` in `Vehicle` interface, shown in the following snippet:

```java
// InheritingBehaviour.java

// Engine interface returning default make
interface Engine {
  default String make(){
    return "DEFAULT MAKE";
  }
}

// Vehicle interface returning default model
interface Vehicle {
  default String model(){
    return "DEFAULT MODEL";
  }
}
```

Now, we wish to combine these two functionalities to produce a `Car` inheriting from `Engine` and `Vehicle` interfaces:

```
// InheritingBehaviour.java

class Car implements Engine, Vehicle{
  public String getMakeAndModel(){
    return Engine.super.make()+":"+Vehicle.super.model();
  }
}
```

Suppose, we have a `Car` object implementing both Engine and Vehicle functionality inheriting from these two separate interfaces. What we are doing is using the default behaviour - the behaviour defined in two completely independent interfaces, into a `Car` object., which is nothing but a mechanism of inheriting behaviour from multiple interfaces. It may look a simple thing at first glance, but considering the taboo around multiple-inheritance in Java, it is actually a big change in our mind set since its introduction in Java 8.

Inheriting multiple-state is still a no-no in Java. We know the multiple inheritance of state is evil and hence no place in Java since its beginnings. The dreaded diamond shape inheritance (multiple inheritance of state) problem has been out of picture in Java right from day one.

Imagine how we would have done if we don't have default methods? Well, it was impossible as Java wouldn't allow multiple inheritance strategy. Note that what we are inheriting is simply a behaviour or a functionality but not state.

Multiple Inheritance

We learned that with the use of default methods we can support multiple inheritance of behaviour in our applications. However, there is a case when interfaces with same method definitions exists. There are some rules that must be taken into account in order to understand the concept of multiple inheritance.

Inheritance Rules

Let's start understanding the rules that govern inheritance in Java. We take a simple case of a `Doctor` and a `Surgeon` each operating patients. The interface definitions are given below:

```
// InheritanceRules.java

// A general practitioner operating on a patient
interface Doctor{
  default String operate(Patient p){
  return "Patient operated by a general physician";
  }
}

// A consultant operating a patient
interface Surgeon{
  default String operate(Patient p){
    return "Patient is being operated by a specialist";
  }
}
```

and the Hospital class which implements Doctor interface. The Hospital calls the Doctor to operate the patient as the following example explains:

```
// InheritanceRules.java

// A hospital implementing Doctor functional interface
class Hospital implements Doctor{
  private String admitAndOperate(Patient p){
    // this operate is referring to a super method
    return operate(p);
  }
}
```

As you may have observed, the admitAndOperate method of the Hospital is invoking the operate method inherited from the Doctor interface.

Now, say, we have another interface Surgeon (let's complicate life!), who can operate patients if referred to him/her, has the same method operate as of the Doctor interface:

The definition goes like this:

```
// The interface has exact same method name as Doctor
interface Surgeon{
  default String operate(Patient p){
    return "Patient is being operated by a specialist";
  }
}
```

Looking at the Doctor and Surgeon interfaces, we now know that both are implementing same default method `operate`! What will happen to the `Hospital` object if we implement two interfaces with same method signatures:

```
// InheritanceRules.java

// Class implementing two interfaces which has
// identical methods. The compiler will throw errors.

class Hospital implements Doctor, Surgeon{
  private String admitAndOperate(Patient p){
    return operate(p);
    }
}
```

The code will not compile. The compiler complains that duplicate methods were inherited in this class. We confused the compiler and it doesn't know which method the class needs to use as both are same and there's no precedence of one over the other. In other words, the compiler can't make a decision for you.

In such situations, it is we who should be giving clear instructions and dictating a direction. There are fundamentally two rules that we need to follow to resolve such issues, discussed next.

Rule 1: Explicit Declaration

Inheritance Rule 1 states that a class must declare its intention *explicitly by overriding* the default methods.

That is, the `Hospital` class should define a method with same name so it doesn't confuse the compiler. The compiler simply picks up the class's declaration (class may point to use one of the interface's definition). Hence, explicit `Class` declaration always wins.

```
// InheritanceRules.java

// We override the method and provide own implementation
class Hospital implements Doctor, Surgeon{
  // Overriding with own implementation
  public String operate(Patient p){
    return "Patient operated";
  }
}
```

By providing a custom implementation, we have duplicated the method in

57

the class. Unfortunately there is nothing we could do in this scenario.

However, if we know we can use either of the interface's `default` method, then simply use the `super` keyword to grab the method from the respective super interface. For example, in our `Hospital2` class, we let the general practitioner (`Doctor`) operate the patient, hence we invoke the `Doctor`'s `operate` method:

```
// InheritanceRules.java

// Referring to Doctor's implementation specifically
class Hospital2 implements Doctor, Surgeon{
  public String operate(Patient p){
    return Doctor.super.operate(p);
  }
}
```

Should we wish to use `Surgeon` instead, we can invoke `Surgeon.super.operate(p)` method.

Did you notice the usage of `super` keyword? It's a new enhancement to the `super` keyword in Java 8. You use invoke the interface's method in the format: `<Interface>.super.<method_name>` as demonstrated in the examples above.

Rule 2: Most Specific Interfaces Wins

In our `Hospital` case, we have both `Doctor` and `Surgeon` performing operations independently. However, consider a case where one of them inherits the behaviour from the other. For example, our `Doctor` extending the `Surgeon` interface, like below, overriding the `operate` method:

```
// InheritanceRules2.java

// Interface extending the other and overriding the method
interface Doctor extends Surgeon{
  default String operate(Patient p){
    return "Patient operated by a general physician";
  }
}
```

In this case, we certainly can expect `Hospital` class implementing *both* these interfaces. The compiler is not going to throw tantrums. At the same time, the `Hospital` expects the operation being performed by `Doctor` but not `Surgeon` (although it inherits `Surgeon` which has an `operate` method of its own). See the perfectly valid code snippet shown below:

```java
// InheritanceRules2.java

// Class  implements  two  interfaces  but  one  interface
extends the other

public class Hospital implements Doctor, Surgeon{
  public String admitAndOperate(Patient p){
    // Invokes Doctor's operate method
    return operate(p);
  }
}
```

This is because of the second rule: Sub-interfaces are winners i.e. the method from closest ancestor will be selected. In this case, Doctor is the closest in the hierarchy graph (remember, Doctor extends Surgeon) to a Hospital object, and hence the Doctor implementation gets picked by the compiler.

Finally (as a third rule), if neither of the above rules resolve our conflicts, we

---

If a class provides an implementation, it will be the first choice by the compiler. If not the sub-interface's most specific (closest ancestor) method is chosen. Else, our own implementation would take precedence over everything else.

---

need to resolve it explicitly by overriding the implementations in the class. It is the responsibility of the developer to sort this issue rather depending on multiple inheritance feature.

Intersection Types

Java 8 has a very interesting feature of creating a new type by intersecting other types. This new type is called an *intersecting type* and can be put to a useful work when working with Lambdas.

For example, should you wish to serialise a lambda expression, how would we do that? That is, how can we extend our lambda expression with a Serializable interface. Or may be a lambda expression that would be tagged with a faster random access as delivered by a RandomAccess marker interface?

The *intersection types* will come to our rescue in satisfying such requirements. Take an example of a Shape interface with no methods - hence this acts as a marker interface.

```
// IntersectionTypes.java

// Marker interface (no methods)
interface Shape{ }
```

Now, say a `Ball` interface is an interface that has single abstract method bounce.

```
// IntersectionTypes.java

// A ball that bounces
interface Ball {
  void bounce();
}
```

It is the right candidate to be a target type of a lambda expression, hence we can create a lambda expression, as shown below:

```
// IntersectionTypes.java

// A lambda expression for the bouncing ball
Ball b = () -> print("Bouncing..");
```

If our intention is to create a lambda expression that's a ball as well as a shape, (that is, a cross between `Ball` and a `Shape`), how do we do that?

We can use the intersection type to create a cross between the interfaces to produce a new breed. So, if we have two types `T1` and `T2`, we can create a new type by simply intersecting them by joining them with an ampersand (`&`) like this: (`T1&T2`)

In our example, what we need to do is to intersect `Ball` and `Shape` so `Ball` can now become a `Shape` too. The following snippet performs this function:

```
//Intersection type between Ball and Shape
Ball ball =
  (Ball & Shape)() -> print("Bouncing shape..");
```

Note that the lambda expression is type casted to this new type (highlighted code), that results in a functional interface which is a `Ball` *and a* `Shape`.

Serializing Lambdas

We can use the same technique of intersection typing to serialiaze a lambda too. Say we wish to serialize the lambda expression representing `Ball` functional interface. We cross our `Ball` with `Serializable` interface as shown here:

```
Ball serializableBallLambda =
 (Ball&Serializable)()->print("Serializable ball");
```

The `serializableBallLambda` lambda is a candidate for persistence using Java serialization method.

However, one thing you need to keep in mind. The target type yielding from such intersections should be a functional interface if our intention is to use it in the context of a lambda expression. In the above case, `Ball` is the functional interface and hence the lambda expression is assigned to a `Ball` type.

Summary

In this chapter, we looked at the evolution and revolution of interfaces. We found that interfaces can have concrete methods (`static` and `default` methods). We learned about the inheriting behaviours as well as multiple inheritance strategies. We also explored the inheritance rules resolving method conflicts during multiple inheritance implementations. We finally looked at the intersection types which are a cross between two interfaces.

7. FUNCTIONS

Java 8 introduced a functions library with many functions available off the shelf representing recurring functionalities such as checking for a condition, supplying a list of values, consuming inputs, transforming a type to another type and others. In this chapter, we look at these functions in detail.

Introducing Functions

It is boring to do the same type of task over and over again. Many times we may have a recurring functionality being added to our application such as a function for finding a customer, or a function to book a reservation etc. Sometimes, there may have been duplicated functions sprinkled around the projects, for example one application retrieving the customer details for order placement, while another application posting marketing promotions. These two applications are actually dependent on the same requirement (finding the customer). It would be wise to create a single *find-a-customer* function that can be used by these two applications (in fact any application) rather than repeating the logic in every individual project.

Thinking on an abstract one level up, checking for a valid condition, transforming one type to another type, consuming an input for some internal processing or publishing a response for an inbound request are functionalities that recur over and over again.

Look at the following functional interfaces which checks for a condition on a given input:

```
// RecurringFunctions.java

// Check if the movies belongs to thriller genre
interface Movie{
  boolean isThriller(int movieId);
}

// Get an employee given an id
interface Employee{
  Employee fetch(int empId);
}

// Admit the patient
interface Hospital{
  void admit(Patient patient);
}

// Supply  the properties required to seed the system
interface Seeder{
 List<Properties> seed(String system);
}
```

If we look at these interfaces and the features they are supporting closely, we can see a common strategy repeating itself. For example, consider the Movie interface: given an id, it checks for a condition and returns true or false - in essence it is a *function for conditional checking*. Similarly, the Employee maps an id to an Employee - a *function producing an output*. Or, a Hospital designed to admit a patient - a *function that accepts inputs* possibly for further processing. Lastly, Seeder is the function that produces application initialisation data - *a function for supplying data*.

Sure we may have umpteen cases like this in our applications. Instead of creating a set of interfaces for each and every case or type, wouldn't it be better if we have generalised interfaces that would be used irrespective of the use cases? For example, we may create a Producer for producing data or Consumer for consumption of data or other in-house implementations depending on our requirements. See the custom implementations defined defined here below:

```java
// RecurringFunctions.java

// Custom interfaces for checking conditionality
interface Tester<T>{
  boolean test(T t);
}

// Interface for Producing objects
interface Producer<T>{
  T produce(int id);
}

// Interface for consuming elements
interface Consumer<T>{
  void consume(T t);
}
```

Well, fortunately, that is what Java 8 has done for us by creating a library of functions. Instead of creating a plethora of our own functions, the language has provided handful of them via its functions library. The common functionalities are captured by Java 8's new functions library.

Functions Library

The functions library encompasses various functions - functions for conditional checking, consuming data, mapping a data point to another, transforming one type to another etc. For example, the functionality of testing for a valid condition is defined in a Predicate interface.

Besides Predicate, other interfaces such as Consumer, Function and Supplier along with many variants of these interfaces were created. We usually call this library as *Functions Library*. A new package called java.util.function was created to house these new functions. Let's dive into learning them in the next few sections.

Predicate Function

If our intention is to test a boolean expression, e.g. to check if a given employee can receive bonus for his good work, if a room is available in a hotel, if the computer is running slow etc, then we can use the Predicate function. The aim of the Predicate function is to evaluate a condition for returning true or false.

The Predicate interface definition is shown here:

```
@FunctionalInterface
public interface Predicate<T> {
  // single abstract method
  boolean test(T t);

  // Other methods such as and, or & negate
  ....
}
```

As you can see, the `Predicate` is a generic interface having a single abstract method named `test`. The `test` methods evaluates the given arguments and returns a `true` or `false` based on some conditional checks. There are other methods defined in this interface too which we will look at them shortly.

Let's see the usage of `Predicate` in action. We need to check if an employee is eligible for a bonus package by evaluating employee's performance against a rating criteria. The logic is not important here but understanding the usage of `Predicate` is.

Let's create a lambda expression for this condition:

```
// Predicates.java

// Does the Employee has enough rating
Predicate<Employee> bonusEligibleLambda =
  emp -> emp.getRatings() > 10;
```

Given an employee as an input to this lambda expression, it returns a boolean value. Notice the return type - it's a Java 8's `Predicate` type. This functionality fits the `Predicate` requirement of conditional checking, hence the lambda is assigned to a `Predicate`. So any function that can check for a condition returning `boolean` result can be defined using `Predicate` function going forward.

We can create any required number of predicates depending on our requirements. For example, the following snippets are all `Predicate` functions checking a boolean condition:

```
// Predicates.java

// Is the patient seriously ill?
Triage t = patient -> patient.isSerious();

// Is the given string empty?
Predicate<String> emptyString = s -> s.isEmpty();

// Is out trade in open status?
Predicate<Trade> openTrade = t -> t.isOpen();
```

We don't have to use our bespoke interfaces for a boolean valued single argument functions anymore. Remember, for checking the open trade, we used to use our own interface? See below for a glimpse of how we can start using functions library:

```
// Custom functional interface for checking an open trade
ITrade openTrade = t -> t.isOpen();

// The same using function's library
Predicate<Trade> openTrade = t -> t.isOpen();
```

There are other methods exposed on the `Predicate` interface such as negate, and and or methods for checking other functionalities. We use these methods to chain several predicates to create a complex conditional algorithm. This process is called functional composition. We will learn about composition of functions in the next chapter.

Consumer Function

Similar to a `Predicate` functional interface, Java 8 provides a `Consumer` function for accepting an input and returning nothing (void). `Consumer` interface is a generic interface that has a single abstract method `accept` along with a default method called `andThen` too.

The interface definition is presented here:

```
// Consumer functional interface

interface Consumer<T>{
  // Single abstract method of the functional interface
  void accept(T t);

  //default andThen method..
}
```

The `accept` method accepts a single argument and returns `void`. So, any functionality like persisting an object, encrypting a file, deleting an entry in the database, etc., are good candidates for `Consumer` function, of course as long as we don't expect return from these methods.

Let's start with a simple example of persisting the movie information to a durable storage. As this functionality returns nothing, `Consumer` is the good fit. Our lambda expression using `Consumer` as the type looks like this:

```
// Consumers.java

// A lambda with Consumer target type
Consumer<Movie> persistMovie = this::persist;

// Using an existing instance method to persist the movie
private void persist(Movie m) {
  System.out.println("Persisting "+m);
}

// Test it

// Invoking the accept method will execute persist method
persistMovie.accept(movie);
```

We are using an existing method persist which does the job of storing the movie information to a database. Once we have the lambda expression ready, we can put it into action by simply invoking the `accept` method on the lambda by passing a `Movie` object.

Supplier Function

The `Supplier` function is a candidate to supply the user with some data. If we may need to seed our application with initial set of data or configuration properties, `Supplier` is the function to do so.. It's the opposite of the `Consumer` function in a sense that it doesn't take any input arguments but returns data out.

The interface definition looks like this:

```
// Supplier interface definition
@FunctionalInterface
public interface Supplier<T> {
  T get();
}
```

It is a generic interface with one method `get` which expects no inputs but returns same type. `Supplier` can be used as function for seeding data.

We may want to load a list of employees in our application cache, fetching some newly created trades, or simply getting some default configurational values of a customer. These requirements are well suited for `Supplier` function.

Say, we want to create a drinks-query service, a service that responds with a list of soft drinks for anyone querying it. We create a `Supplier` of drinks so a client wishing to retrieve drinks, she can simply ask the supplier. Let's create the lambda representing a supplier to fetch a list of drinks (drinks are supplied as a `List` of `Strings`):

```java
// Suppliers.java

// A supplier supplying list of drinks

Supplier<List<String>> drinksSupplier = () -> {
  List<String> drinks = new ArrayList<String>();

  drinks.add("Orange Juice");
  drinks.add("Pineapple");
  drinks.add("Custard Apple");

  return drinks;
};
```

The above code simply creates a local store of drinks (ideally it should have been retrieved from a durable storage), returning to the user when asked for. Once we have the supplier, we can invoke the `get` method on the supplier which fetches the result, as demonstrated here:

```java
// Suppliers.java

// Fetching the drinks from the supplier
public void getDrinks(){
  List<String> softDrinks = drinksSupplier.get();
  softDrinks.stream().forEach(System.out::println);
}
```

We browse through the drinks list one by one printing them to the console.

`Supplier` is a good candidate for fetching data in to our applications. It doesn't need any inputs but returns the results to a client. Unlike `Predicate` or `Consumer`, it doesn't have any `static` or `default` methods.

`Function` Function

There may be some instances where we wish to fetch a result for a given input. For example, given an employee id, we like to retrieve an employee, or may be transforming temperature from Centigrade to Fahrenheit, or perhaps searching for an exception Java programmer across the nation!

This type of requirement is supported by the `Function` functional interface - when given an input returns a result. Before we jump into understanding the `Function`, let's see the interface definition:

```
// Functions.java

public interface Function<T, R> {
  R apply(T t);
  // other default and static methods
  ....
}
```

The interface has a single abstract method called `apply` which consumes an object of type `T` producing a type `R` in return. The `apply` method applies the logic on the input argument to produce the result.

Let's take a simple example: given a movie name, we wish to create a `Movie` and return it (movie name is a `String` object while the returned result is a type of `Movie`).

We can express this requirement using a `Function`:

```
// Function that given a string, returns a movie
Function<String, Movie> movieFunction =
  movieName -> new Movie(movieName);
```

Notice the function's argument generic types. The `String` and `Movie` represents the input and output respectively. Hence, it's saying 'provide me a title and I'll give you a movie'. Once the function is created, using it is quite straight forward:

```
// Use our movie function to create a Movie
Movie movie = movieFunction.apply(movieName);

System.out.println("Movie created:"+movie);
```

Let's take another example. This time, we wish to find a trade from a list of trades. The input is an `Integer` (the id of the trade), and return is a `Trade`. So our function can be written as:

```java
// Functions.java

List<Trade> trades = ....;

Function<Integer, Trade> tradeFinder = (id) -> {
   // Run through all the trades
   // checking against the given one
   Trade trade = null;
   for (Trade t : trades) {
     if (t.getId() == id)
        trade = t;
     }
     return trade;
   };
// invoke it
public void tradeFinder(Integer id) {
   Trade trade = tradeFinder.apply(id);
   System.out.println("Fetched a trade: "+trade);
}
```

Here, we have a list of trades looping through one by one comparing against a given trade id. If the criteria matches, we return that trade, else return a new trade. Once we have the `Function` created, use its apply method to invoke it, as demonstrated in the above code snippet.

If you are curious, the `for` loop defined above can be re-written in favour of Java 8's streams, as demonstrated below. We will cover streams in due course.

```java
List<Trade> trades = ....;

// Using Java 8 Streams
public void tradeFinderJava8(Integer tradeId) {
   List<Trade> trades = TradeUtil.createTrades();

   Trade trade = trades
     .stream()
     .filter(t -> t.getId() == tradeId)
     .findFirst()
     .get();
   print("Fetched a trade (using Streams): "+trade);
}
```

The `Function` interface is a best fit for situations like mapping, transformations or extractions.

Summary

In this chapter, we discussed the predicate and consumer functions at length. We looked at them in action as well as the mechanism of composing high order functions. We also explored the various static and default methods exposed by these functions.

8. COMPOSING FUNCTIONS

In our earlier chapter, we looked at a set of functions that Java 8 library has to offer. If we have already defined a set of functions, we can compose them together to execute a complex business function. In this chapter, we learn about the mechanism of function composition in detail.

Composing Predicates

If you look at the `Javadoc` for the `Predicate` interface, there are a few more methods other than the single abstract method `test` in there. These additional methods allow us to create more complex lambda expressions.

Say we have two `Predicate` functions representing a big trade and a cancelled trade:

```
// Lambda expression for a big trade
Predicate<Trade> bigTrade = t -> t.isBigTrade();

// Lambda expression for a cancelled trade
Predicate<Trade> cancelledTrade =
  t -> t.isCancelledTrade();
```

However, if we have a requirement of finding a big trade with a cancelled status, we can chain the two individual functions together rather than creating a new `Predicate` which may have duplicated logic from the existing functions. Hence sensible thing to do is to chain the existing `Predicates` to build a newly composed predicate. And this is where those extra methods on the `Predicate` interface come into picture.

Using and Method

The and method is used to compose and create a new `Predicate` from existing predicates. It is a default method accepting a `Predicate` returning a `Predicate` by applying logic supplied by individual predicates. It applies a logical AND on the given two input predicates.

Let's understand working through out example. Using an and method, we compose a new `Predicate` for cancelled *and* big trade, as demonstrated here below:

```
// Predicates.java

// Existing functions
Predicate<Trade> cancelledTrade = Trade::isCancelledTrade;
Predicate<Trade> bigTrade =Trade::isBigTrade;

// A cancelled & big trade predicate
Predicate<Trade>
  cancelledAndBigTrade = cancelledTrade.and(bigTrade);
```

Make a note that the composed function gets evaluated if and only if the trade is cancelled. If the first function evaluates to be false (that is, the trade is not cancelled), the second expression (big trade function) doesn't get executed (logical AND functionality). We are essentially chaining the predicates as our requirement dictates.

Using or Method

Similar to logical AND, there's another method on the `Predicate` called or which, as the name suggests is used as *logical OR*.

Say we have two predicates each checking the status (new or pending trade) of a trade:

```
// Predicates.java

// Predicate for NEW status
Predicate<Trade> newTrade =  Trade::isNew;

// Predicate for PENDING status
Predicate<Trade> pendingTrade = Trade::isPending;
```

For checking a condition representing either a new trade or a pending one, we use the logical OR on our existing two lambdas to create a new piece of functionality checking for either of the condition:

```
// Predicates.java

// Either new or pending trade
Predicate<Trade> orLambda = newTrade.or(pendingTrade);
```

This lambda checks if the status of the trade is NEW. If first predicate evaluates to true it does not need to evaluate the second one. Similar to and composing predicates, there's no restriction on how many functions to chain.

Mixing and & or Methods

We can also mix both logical AND and logical OR predicates too. Using the earlier predicates, for example, checking for a trade if it's new or pending but large, can be defined as shown here:

```
// Predicates.java

// New or pending but big trade
Predicate<Trade> newOrPendingButBigTrade =
newTrade.or(pendingTrade).and(bigTrade);
```

Using negate and isEqual Methods

The negate method can be used to check for an inverse condition. For example, if we wish to find out if the trade is anything but a new trade, we simply invoke negate on the newTrade predicate:

```
// Predicates.java

// We know there's a predicate for new trade:
//And this becomes a predicate for anything but new:
Predicate<Trade> notNewTrade = newTrade.negate();
```

Lastly, there is a static method on the Predicate interface called isEqual for comparing two objects. If we want to compare each of the trades against an issuer such as GOOGLE, we do this as shown in the predicate below.

```
// Predicates.java

// Reference trade
Trade t1 = new Trade("GOOGLE", 200000, "CANCEL");

// Predicate to check the trade against reference trade
Predicate<Trade> p1 = Predicate.isEqual(t1);

// Predicate which compares the given trades
for(Trade t: trades){
  if(p1.test(t)){
    System.out.println("Found a matching trade: "+t);
  }
}
```

We created a `Predicate` by using a `isEqual` method with a reference GOOGLE trade to compare against. When we have the list of trades, loop through the list to find out the matching trade. Rather than using the traditional for look, we can use Java 8's stream functionality too like `trades.stream().anyMatch(p1)` which we will study in due course.

Composing Consumers

Similar to what we have learned about composing `Predicates`, we can also compose(chain) the `Consumers` using `andThen` default method. The `andThen` method invokes the current consumer first and then invokes the second consumer afterwards.

Consider an example of auditing movie information before persisting it to a durable storage. If we already have existing lambdas for these functionalities (auditing and persisting), all we have to do is to compose them using `andThen` such that we log the movie information for audit purposes first before persisting the movie. This is demonstrated in the following code segment:

```
// Consumer for auditing movie
Consumer<Movie> auditMovie = this::audit;

// Consumer for persisting movie
Consumer<Movie> persistMovie = this::persist;

// The composed consumer auditing and persisting a movie
Consumer<Movie> andThenConsumer =
  auditMovie.andThen(persistMovie);

// Test it: Invoke the consumer by passing a movie
andThenConsumer.accept(movie);
```

Note that sequencing of the functions when using the `andThen` method. It first invokes the `accept` on the first consumer (`auditMovie`), followed by the second consumer (`persistMovie`), that is, it audits the movie before persisting it to a durable storage.

Chaining the Consumers

We can also chain the consumers to form a single consumer with all the functional requirements knitted together. Consider the lambda expression below that distributes the movie to a certain region:

```
// Consumers.java

Consumer<Movie> distribute = t -> distribute(t);

private void distribute(Movie m) {
  System.out.println("Distributing "+m);
}
```

We can compose all three lambdas by daisy-chaining the three actions of audit, persistence and distribution together, as shown below:

```
// Create the chained consumer
private void ChainingConsumers(Movie movie) {

  // Creating the chained consumer
  Consumer<Movie> chainedConsumer = auditMovie
    .andThen(persistMovie)
    .andThen(distributeMovie);

  // Invoke it
  chainedConsumer.accept(movie);
}
```

Composing Functions

Following the same theme of composition of functions, `Function` will allow us to associate functions together to perform a complex set of actions, i.e., we can chain these functions to design a sequence of functionalities. `Function` functional interface has two default methods: `andThen` and `compose` methods. It also has a `static` method named `identity`.

Using andThen Method

Say we have two functions, a function to fetch a Book title given an ISBN (bookFinder) and another function (rankFinder) returning the sales rank of the book given a Book as the input.

```
// Functions.java

// Function for finding the book given an ISBN
Function<String, Book> bookFinder = this::fetchBook;

// Function finding the rank of the book
Function<Book, Integer> rankFinder = this::rankFinder;
```

If our requirement is to find a book's sales rank, we can compose these existing functions together to create a new one, as shown here:

```
// Functions.java

// A function returning the sales rank given an ISBN
Function<String, Integer>
   bookRankFinder = bookFinder.andThen(rankFinder);
```

The bookFinder function will be put into action first, so the outcome from this action is a Book. The second function rankFinder is then invoked passing the result obtained from the first function (Book) as the input argument. The rankFinder will use the book as its input to search and return the sales rank of the book. So, all in all, given an ISBN, the book's sales rank can fetched.

Make a note of the order of functions when using andThen method. The bookFinder is invoked first followed by the rankFinder. The return type of the andThen function might be of some interest which is discussed in the next section.

Function Types

When it comes to composing Functions, forming a return type becomes a bit complicated. The above function's return type Function<String, Integer> has a bit of a story to reveal.

As we already know, the bookRankFinder lambda is composed of two functions: a bookFinder and rankFinder functions. The bookFinder accepts a String resulting in a Book while the rankFinder consumes a

`Book` producing an `Integer`.

When we compose functions using `andThen`, the output of the first function will be used as the input of the second function. So, the `Book` produced as the result from the `bookFinder` will then be fed into `rankFinder`. This in return produces an `Integer` (sales rank).

If we put all these together, given an ISBN number, we fetch a book and given a book we retrieve its sales rank.

Using compose method

The `compose` method on the `Function` is a more like a reverse of the `andThen` functionality. For example, say we have an interest calculator function which applies certain rate of interest (2% in the following case) on a given amount. Similarly, we may have another function that would apply a factor to a given amount. Both functions are defined below:

```
// Functions.java

// A function to calculate interest on a principal
Function<Integer, Integer>
   interestCalculator = amount -> amount*2;

Function<Integer, Integer>
   factoredInterest = amount -> amount+10;
```

If we wish to calculate interest first and then factor it, we use the `andThen` function as we had seen in previous section. However, if we wish to reverse this condition, that is, factor it and calculate the interest on the factored amount, then we can use `compose` method. For simplicity sake, we are going to compare and contrast both `andThen` and `compose` here. Consider the composed functions defined below:

```
// Functions.java

// Calculate interest followed by factoring it
principalInterest.andThen(factoredInterest).apply(10)

// Factor the principal before calculating interest.
principalInterest.compose(factoredInterest).apply(10)

// Output
Apply interest first before factoring it :30
Factor the amount and then apply interest:40
```

When you execute the program, you see a different result from each of the above functions. For example, andThen function produces an amount of £30 while compose function outputs £40 for the principal of £10!

The ordering of the functions in a compose function is worth a note. The factoredInterest (the argument passed to the compose method) is executed first followed by the principalInterest function (unlike in the andThen function where principalInterest will be invoked first followed by the factoredInterest function).

Using static Method

Lastly, did you notice a static method called identity on the interface? This method is used to return the same output as the input. That is, if we give a string say "ABCD", we get the same output. The input and output types should be declared as the function generic types.

Check the definition of the function (the input and output are of same type T):

```
// Function's identity
static <T> Function<T, T> identity(){
    return t -> t;
}
```

Note that the arguments must be of the same type. Let's walk through an example. We create a function called idFunction, which is assigned an identity, as shown here below:

```
// Functions.java

Function<String, String> idFunction = Function.identity();
String result = idFunction.apply("ISBN123");
```

The static method creates a Function that simply returns the input to the user. The result is nothing but what we've passed in (ISBN123).

Summary

In this chapter, we looked at the ways of composing high order functions. High order functions are well suited in defining complex logic by employing existing function definitions.

9. SPECIALIZED FUNCTIONS

The library functions that we have learned so far were designed to have a single argument. We most likely have cases where the functions need more than one argument. For example, we wish to find the availability of a hotel during two dates; or searching for a book in a library with two inputs (year of publication and classification) and many others. In this chapter, we will explore these bi-arity functions as well as few other advanced function concepts.

Binary Functions

Functions that take two input arguments are called as binary functions.

Take an example of checking if the given manager as input is the employee's manager. We need to provide both employee and manager to deduce this. The return suggests a yes or no answer, that is, a boolean valued expression. As we did earlier, we can use Predicate to check the condition, however Predicate accepts a single argument only. For our requirement, we need a function accepting two arguments returning a boolean. This is where we bring in a two-argument version of predicate called BiPredicate.

Fortunately, Java's function library created a new set of interfaces for satisfying bi-argument requirements. They are BiPredicate, BiConsumer, BiSupplier and BiFunction. As the name suggests, they all work on two input arguments. Let's explore each one of them in the following sections.

BiPredicate Function

BiPredicate is same like it's twin brother Predicate except that it takes two arguments. The definition of `BiPredicate` goes like this:

```
@FunctionalInterface
public interface BiPredicate<T, U> {
  boolean test(T t, U u);
  //other static and default methods
  ....
}
```

The interface is a generic one with two input types, T and U as shown in the above definition, returning a `boolean` as the result. Say, we want to check if two trade identifiers are equal. The function accepts two trades and return a true or false value using a `BiPredicate` function. This is demonstrated in the following code snippet along with few more examples of `BiPredicate` function usage:

```
//BiPredicates.java

// A BiPredicate accepting two trades, returning boolean
BiPredicate<Trade, Trade>
  tradeComparer = (t1, t2) -> t1.getId() == t1.getId();


// Or BiPredicate for comparing strings
BiPredicate<String, String>
  stringComparer = (s1, s2) -> s1.equalsIgnoreCase(s2);

// Function to copy from an encrypted trade
BiPredicate<Trade, EncryptedTrade> tradeCopier = (trade1,
trade2)-> {
  boolean copySuccess = false;
  if(!trade1.isOpen()){
    copySuccess = trade1.copy(trade2);
  }
  return copySuccess;
};
```

Chaining `BiPredicates`

As we did for unary functions, we can also compose the `BiPredicates` to produce a complex function suitable for our business logic. Similar to the three default methods in `Predicate`, an `and` (logical AND), an `or` (logical OR) and a `negate` methods exists in `BiPredicate` too.

The `and` method short circuits the evaluation. Suppose we have a `empManagerPredicate`, a `BiPredicate` function to check the manager of an employee given both and employee and a manager.

In addition to this predicate, say we have another function, the `mgrHasAssistantPredicate`, which checks if the personal assistant of the given manager is also an employee.

```
// BiPredicates.java

// These two predicates execute different functions
BiPredicate<Employee, Manager> empManagerPredicate =
  (emp, manager) ->  emp.getManager().equals(manager);

BiPredicate<Employee, Manager> mgrHasAssistantPredicate=
(emp,manager)->manager.getPersonalAssistant().equals(emp);
```

Given an employee, we need to check out his/her manager first *and* check if the employee is manager's personal assistant too. This is demonstrated in the code snippet below where two predicates are associated using and method:

```
// BiPredicates.java

// Composed function using and method
BiPredicate<Employee, Manager> isPersonalAssistant =
empManagerPredicate.and(mgrHasAssistPredicate);
```

The application of the function ordering is important. The first function (`empManagerPredicate`) will be evaluated first before moving on to evaluate the second one (`mgrHasAssistPredicate`).

Following the same lines, it isn't a rocket science to understand the logical OR method. If we wish to find out if the employee has a manager *or* if the employee is assistant to the manager, then we simply create a `BiPredicate` using the logical OR method:

```
// BiPredicates.java

// Using OR method
BiPredicate<Employee, Manager> isPersonalAssistant =
empManagerPredicate.or(mgrHasAssistPredicate);
```

Lastly, there's a `negate` default method defined on the interface which is used if we wish to find an inverse of a condition. If we want to find out if the given employee *does not* have the same manager that we have passed in, we can negate the existing predicate (`empManagerPredicate`) as shown:

```
//BiPredicates.java

//Negating the existing predicate
BiPredicate<Employee, Manager> notAManagerPredicate =
empManagerPredicate.negate();
```

BiConsumer Function

Two argument `BiConsumer` function has no surprises. As the name suggests, it consumes the two arguments that we pass to it (returns nothing). Checkout the definition of `BiConsumer` interface given below:

```
public interface BiConsumer<T, U> {
  void accept(T t, U u);
  // other default methods
}
```

As you can see, the `BiConsumer` accepts two arguments of type `T` and `U` returning void.

For example, we want to apply a percentage of bonus for a hard working employee (like you!). We can write a `BiConsumer` function for this purpose as shown in the following code example:

```
// BiConsumers.java

BiConsumer<Employee, Integer> empBonusConsumer =
(emp, bonus) -> printf("Employee %s with %d pct of bonus",
emp, bonus);
```

The inputs to this function are an employee and his/her bonus figure. The lambda expression is using both these arguments to derive a final figure of remuneration to the employee (although a simple print statement here). In a sense, the `Consumer` function is operating using side-effects.

andThen Method

A default method `andThen` is defined on the `BiConsumer` interface. This method is used to compose a `BiConsumer` function using two existing other `BiConsumer` functions. Say, in addition to the above `empBonusConsumer`, we may have another one, a salary hike consumer function:

```
// BiConsumers.java

// A salary hike function (two inputs)
BiConsumer<Employee, Integer> empSalHikeConsumer =
(emp, manager) -> printf("\nEmployee %s is receiving %d
hike in salary", emp,manager);
```

Now that we have these two functions, if we want to apply bonus
percentage *and* salary hike to the given employee (really hard working
employee!), we can use these two lambda expressions to compose them
using the andThen function:

```
// BiConsumers.java

// Using andThen method
BiConsumer<Employee, Integer> empBonusAndHikeConsumer =
empBonusConsumer.andThen(empSalHikeConsumer);
```

The empBonusConsumer will be evaluated first with the given arguments.
The result of the empBonusConsumer function is then passed on to the
second consumer function empSalHikeConsumer, which will then be
evaluated to produce a final result.

BiFunction

The two argument variation for a Function is called as BiFunction with
an apply method accepting two parameters:

```
@FunctionalInterface
public interface BiFunction<T, U, R> {
  R apply(T t, U u);
  // default methods here
  ....
}
```

The BiFunction deals with three types: two types T and U are the input
argument types while R is the type of the argument that's returned back to
the user.

Going with the employee-manager problem, suppose we wish to find out
personal assistant of a Manager, given an employee and manager. We can
do this   by creating a lambda expression as shown below (I agree, the
example is a bit weird!):

```
// BiFunctions.java

// BiFunction function definition
BiFunction<Employee,Manager,Employee>  empManagerBiFunction =
(emp, manager) ->{
  Employee employee = null;
  if(emp.getManager().equals(manager))
    employee = manager.getPersonalAssistant();
    return employee;
}
```

The function definition declares three types as generic types - the Employee
and Manager being the input arguments to the function and the last of the
arguments indicating the return type, in this case Employee type is expected
to be returned from the method.

We are using the employee to get his manager and compare against the
input argument before finding out the assistant. As assistant itself is an
Employee, the return type matches to the BiFunction's expectation.

andThen Method

The BiFunction too has a default method called andThen to support
higher-order functions. We can use this method to chain the various
BiFunctions together.

However, there's one thing we need to note: when composing the *single-
argument* functions, the result of the first function flows into the second
function smoothly. This works wonderfully well in those single argument
functions. But, when it comes to a two-argument function, the second
function to be chained expects two arguments while the first function
produces a single argument as output.   That is, the second function is
always expects a single argument (single argument Function). See the
definition of the andThen below:

```
// andThen function definition

default <V> BiFunction<T, U, V> andThen(Function after) {
  ...
}
```

From the definition, we can deduce that the argument that andThen expects
is a Function.To create a chained composite for our BiFunction
function, we need a single argument Function defined too, as shown here:

```
//BiFunctions.java

// Single argument function
Function<Employee, Employee> empManagerFunction =
emp -> emp.getManager().getPersonalAssistant();
```

The gist of the above function is that we fetch employee's manager given an employee and subsequently retrieve the personal assistant of the manager. Now that we have both a `BiFunction` and a `Function`, we can compose them and create a new function:

```
// BiFunctions.java

// Using andThen method
BiFunction<Employee, Manager, Employee> personalAssistant=
empManagerBiFunction.andThen(empManagerFunction);
```

Specilized Functions

Sometimes we may have to pass in same type of inputs to functions, of Designers have created plethora of them. We learn the fundamentals of them here by understanding the specialisations.

Same Type Functions

We know, a `Function` works when given an input of a type T, returns a result of type R. We explicitly define the function with two types, one for the input and other for the output.

Consider a case where the types of the function operands are the same, for example a function consuming an `Integer` and returning an `Integer`, shown below:

```
// SpecializedFunctions.java

Function<Integer, Integer> tradeQuantityLambda = id -> {
   .. ..
   return tradeQuantity;
};
```

As you may have noted, the input-output arguments are of the same type (`Integer and Integer`) for the above function. Wouldn't be better to drop the redundant declaration of the types from the function? Here is where another specialisation of `Function` emerges in the form of

86

UnaryOperator.

UnaryOperator

The UnaryOperator is a specialisation of a one-argument Function, which works on same typed input and output arguments. It extends the Function interface as it is clearly a custom version of Function. See the definition here:

```
public interface UnaryOperator<T> extends Function<T, T> {
  //....
}
```

We can modify our earlier function using the UnaryOperator to take advantage of same-type specialization:

```
private UnaryOperator<Integer> unaryOperator = (id) -> {
  ....
  return tradeQuantity;
};
```

The only difference is that we dropped the extra Integer argument in the function declaration. Following the same pattern, BinaryOperator is a function with two same type arguments.

BinaryOperator Function

The BinaryOperator is a specialisation of BiFunction that operates on two operands of same type resulting in a return value of same type too.

```
interface BinaryOperator<T> extends BiFunction<T,T,T> {
  ..
}
```

Say, for example we wish to write up a function to add quantities of two trades (integer inputs), producing a sum of the both as result(an integer). As all the arguments including the return type are of the same type (integer), we can using BinaryOperator in place of a BinaryFunction, as the following code snippet demonstrates:

```
// SpecialisedFunctions.java

// Function accepting same types and returning same type
BinaryOperator<Integer> sumOfQuantities =
    (quantity1, quantity2) -> quantity1+quantity2;

// invoke the operator with the trade quantities
int result = sumOfQuantities.apply(30000, 44000);
System.out.println(result);

// Output
Sum total: 74000
```

Primitive Specializations

The functions we've seen so far work with reference types but not primitives. We need to employ boxing (or unboxing) for these functions to work with int, boolean, double etc., types.

Consider a predicate that checks if a given integer is an even number.

```
// SpecialisedFunctions.java#checkEvenNumber

Predicate<Integer> evenNumber = (x) -> x % 2 == 0;

// Testing the lambda
print("Is the number even?: "+evenNumber.test(number));
```

Here, we defined a Predicate<Integer> which boxes up the input implicitly, making the type to be a reference type (Integer class in this case). Boxing operation is a tad bit heavy on the performance scale. The objects will be created on the heap which may well add to the memory of our application.

IntPredicate *function*

If we know that we are passing a primitive int, we can abandon the reference type Predicate and instead employ a specialised function called IntPredicate. As the name suggests, this function is the best fit when working with primitive integers. The good news is that the semantics are exactly same as Predicate function, including the static and default methods, hence no steep learning curve!

Let's rewrite the same even number function written above, this time using IntPredicate:

```
// SpecialisedFunctions.java#checkUsingIntPredicate
IntPredicate evenNumber = (x) -> x%2==0;

// Testing the lambda
evenNumber.test(9898);
```

First thing you may have noticed is that we have dropped the type generics from the equation. As you know, the interface is not a generic type, but the name itself gives us the clue that function works with primitive integers only.

Going with the same pattern, we can also have `DoublePredicate` and `LongPredicates` as the specialised versions of `Predicate` for `double` and `long` primitives respectively. See here an example for each of them:

```
// SpecialisedFunctions.java

// Other specialised predicates
private DoublePredicate doublePredicate = x -> x*0.01 < 1;
private LongPredicate longPredicate = x -> x < 10;
```

The primitive functions don't stop with predicates. There are similar specialisations available for the `Consumer`, `Supplier` and `Function` too, which we discuss in our next section. As it is easy to understand these variants, I wouldn't go into details.

Int/Double/Long Consumer function

The `IntConsumer` is a specialisation of the consumer function for primitive `ints`. Likewise, the `DoubleConsumer` is a primitive function for `doubles` and `LongConsumer` for primitive `longs`. See the following code snippet demonstrating simple examples of each of these functions:

```
// SpecialisedFunctions.java#specialisedConsumers

IntConsumer intConsumer = x -> doSomething(x);
intConsumer.accept(10);
DoubleConsumer doubleConsumer =  x -> doSomething(x);
doubleConsumer.accept(20.50);
LongConsumer longConsumer =  x -> doSomething(x);
longConsumer.accept(1001);
```

Int/Double/LongSupplier function

Supplier variants do say the same story as well. IntSupplier returns primitive ints, LongSupplier supplies primitive longs and DoubleSupplier a primitive double value. Look at the following examples demonstrating the usage of these primitive suppliers:

```
// SpecialisedFunctions.java#specialisedSuppliers

IntSupplier intSupplier= () -> 2;
int value = intSupplier.getAsInt();
print("Supplier supplied with (int)"+value);

DoubleSupplier doubleSupplier =  () -> Math.PI;
double piValue = doubleSupplier.getAsDouble();
print("Supplier supplied with (double)"+piValue);

LongSupplier lognSupplier =  () -> 1001;
long longValue = lognSupplier.getAsLong();
print("Supplier supplied with (long) "+longValue);
```

Int/Double/LongFunction function

The IntFunction is a specialization of a Function for primitive ints. The three types of Functions that exist for primitives are IntFunction, DoubleFunction and LongFunction. But there's a twist.

Going with the same storey, When it comes to working with functions, the expectation is that the primitives are provided to the function implicitly. and hence we will not declare them on the method declaration.

Say we have a function that returns an employee given an integer id. Ideally we will define the functions like this:

```
// SpecialisedFunctions.java#specialisedFunctions

// Using a non-primitive friendly function
Function<Integer, Employee> empFunction = null;
```

However, using the IntFunction definition, the above lambda becomes:

```
// SpecialisedFunctions.java#specialisedFunctions

// Converting to a specialised function
IntFunction<Employee> empFunction2 = null;
```

The `IntFunction<Employee>` is the specialised version of `Function` for int. The functions defines that `Employee` is the output while `int` is the input (implicit). Similarly, in a `DoubleFunction`, the `double` is the implicit parameter and same case with `LongFunction` too - given a `long` primitive input, function returns a typed result. See couple of examples shown here:

```
SpecialisedFunctions.java#specialisedFunctions

// A double is provided and a String is returned
DoubleFunction<String> doubleFunction =
  d -> "PI is "+d;  doubleFunction.apply(3.14);

// Given a long id, a Patient is returned
LongFunction<Patient> longFunction =
  id -> new Patient(id);
```

Primitive to Primitive Functions

Lastly, there is another case of a function accepting primitives of one type but returning another type. For example, a function accepting a `int` and returning an `double`, or a function receiving a `long` and returning a `double` and so on and so forth. This is nothing but converting a primitive to another primitive. Instead of creating boxed up `Functions` that employs boxing/unboxing feature, Java designers created another set of customised list of functions for converting primitives to primitives. For example, a `IntToDoubleFunction` accepts an `int` and returns a `double` while `DoubleToIntFunction` does exactly the opposite (accepting a `double` and retuning an `int`). Find some examples of such function below:

```
// SpeciaisedFunctions.java#primitiveConversionFunctions

// Returning a rounded number
LongToIntFunction f = x -> Math.round(x);
// Given a double value, return an integer
DoubleToIntFunction f = x -> 1;

IntToLongFunction intToLongFunction = id -> {
  // prepare an encrypted id
  long encryptedId = 385038204;
  return encryptedId;
};
```

The type generics in not required anymore as the name gives away the intention of the function. Note that the method name follows a pattern like `applyAsXXX`, as listed in the following table:

`DoubleToIntFunction`	Converts double to int	`applyAsInt`
`DoubleToLongFunction`	Converts double to long	`applyAsLong`
`IntToDoubleFunction`	Converts int to double	`applyAsDouble`
`IntToLongFunction`	Converts int to long	`applyAsLong`
`LongToDoubleFunction`	Converts long to double	`applyAsDouble`
`LongToIntFunction`	Converts long to int	`applyAsInt`

Unitype Primitive Operators

We explored some specialized forms of functions like `UnaryOperator` and `BinaryOperators` earlier which are uni-type functions for object references. However, what if our uni-typed arguments are primitives? Of course, the normal functions work for primitives too, but the issue is that they use boxing and unboxing techniques behind the scenes.

To avoid the auto boxing for primitives, functions library has more specializations for primitive types. For example, A `DoubleUnaryOperator` that accepts a single parameter of a double returning a double as its output. Similarly `IntUnaryOperator` and `IntBinaryOperator` works with ints while `LongUnaryOperator` and `LongBinaryOperator` acts on primitive longs.

See the following example snippet demonstrating these operators in action:

```
// SpeciaisedFunctions.java#unitypeSpecialisedFunctions

// Function that operates on a double, returning a double
DoubleUnaryOperator doubleUnaryOperator = d -> d*0.01;
double d = doubleUnaryOperator.applyAsDouble(10);

// Function that accepts an int, returning an int
IntUnaryOperator intUnaryOperator = i -> i*100;
int i = intUnaryOperator.applyAsInt(10);

// Function that accepts a long value, returns a long
LongUnaryOperator longUnaryOperator = l-> l+1;
long l = longUnaryOperator.applyAsLong(10);

System.out.println(d+","+i+", "+l);
```

There are plethora of such specializations and unfortunately, except a few, we will not have time to cover all of them in this book. But trust me they are quite easy to understand if you follow Javadoc.

Summary

In this chapter, we looked at two argument (bi-arity) functions in detail. We also worked through the details of composing and chaining them to prepare higher order functions. We looked at the primitive specializations of these functions too.

10. STREAMS

Java 8 introduced Streams for processing and calculation functionality on data. It is a brand new API with pipeline of operations applying functions on streaming data. In the next few chapters, we will learn all about streams.

Introducing Streams

Imagine a video clip on YouTube or some other online video site. The clip is sitting in a database as one big file somewhere on a server. When you access it, the content is expected to *stream* through to some application for viewing rather than downloading the entire file. The video applications may need to apply some decoding/decrypting functions on this streamed data.

This is what exactly Java 8's Streams API is offering. We can perform functions such as aggregation, filtering, transformations and many others on the streaming data.

Example Using No Streams

Say we have a list of Trades and in this list, we wish to identify those trades with a very large transaction - trades whose value is greater than a million pounds. First let us develop a solution that does not involve streams, but a pre-Java 8 solution, shown below:

```java
// StreamsBasics.java

private List<Trade> findLargeTradesPreJava8(List<Trade>
trades) {
  List<Trade> largeTrades = new ArrayList<Trade>();
  for (Trade trade : trades) {
    if (trade.getQuantity() > ONE_MILLION
        && trade.isCancelledTrade())
      largeTrades.add(trade);
    }
  return largeTrades;
}
```

We begin by creating a new empty collection, an ArrayList to store big trades. Then we iterate through the trades list finding those elements that satisfies the condition (in this case, the quantity of the trade should be greater than one million as well as the trade is cancelled), adding filtered trades to the newly created collection. Once, iteration is over we return the collection.

This is an iterative style of programming that we always used, however there are some inherent problems with this approach which we need to examine.

To begin with, the code is using a throw away (temporary) ArrayList which needless to say can create scalability problem for our application if the list of trades satisfying the condition is very large.

Secondly, the for loop that iterates through the trades list has to be defined *explicitly*. We are actually performing the iteration operation by ourselves. We are not only doing the *how* bit by dictating the loop semantics, we are also performing the *what* bit - i.e., the business logic of what is expected of this iteration.

This brings to an interesting concept of *how versus what*. Why should we bother about the iteration looping while clearly our attention should be focused on the business logic?

Next, we see that the code is written for a single threaded execution model. There are a few moving parts in the code that makes it brittle. Should we wish to paralellize this program, we need to re-engineer the code to make it thread-safe or speed up the performance. Of course, we all are well aware of the difficulties of multi-threading programming. Writing a multithreading correct code is a dark art and is still a dreaded field even for experienced developers.

Last but not least, what if we have to throw in a few more conditions? For example, we like to gather cancelled and large trades, trades against a particular issuer or perhaps trades placed by a trader, and so on. Well, if we follow the imperative programming style, we certainly need to write a lots of control statements using if-else or logical AND/ORs.

This is where the strength of Streams comes into picture.

Example Using Streams

Let us rewrite the previous example, this time using Streams API.

```java
// StreamsBasics.java

private List<Trade> largeTrades(List<Trade> trades){
  return trades
    .stream()
    .filter( trade -> trade.getQuantity() > ONE_MILLION)
    .filter(Trade::isCancelledTrade)
    .collect(Collectors.toList());
}
```

There are lots of things happening here, let's explore them one by one.

The Collection interface has a new method called stream which produces a Stream - a continuous list of elements pouring out from the trades list. The invocation of trades.stream() converts the list of elements into a sequence of elements trade1, trade2, trade3 etc.

The next stage is applying a filter on this stream of elements. Filter is a mechanism of sieving out elements that do not satisfy a condition. In the above code, we wish to select only large trades as well as cancelled. The filter is applied to each element before passing them to the next stage.

Note the filter method accepts a Predicate which checks business conditions returning a boolean value. For each element, the condition is applied, if the condition is satisfied, the element is ushered to the next stage.

The final stage is the process of collecting these elements to a list. We invoke a collect method on the stream by passing a utility method called Collectors.toList which simply collects the elements to an ArrayList.

As you can see, using streams, the code is expressive. It expresses the intent of the developer. There is no intermediate data structure such as a list or a map to collect the resultant elements - at least we don't need to declare one.

One important benefit is out-of-the-box parallelism. We can parallelise the program without stretching a muscle, by invoking the method parallelStream on the collection. See the highlighted code below:

```
// StreamBasics.java

List<Trade> largeTradesParallel(List<Trade> trades){
  return trades
    .parallelStream()
    .filter(trade -> trade.getQuantity() > ONE_MILLION)
    .filter(Trade::isCancelledTrade)
    .collect(Collectors.toList());
}
```

The list will be spilt into sub-lists and send it over to the other cores for multi-processing, finally collecting them to a list. There are a zillion things that happen behind the scenes when we run the program in parallel mode, but good news is that we are spared the details as runtime takes care of everything. We will learn about parallelism in due course.

The last benefit is the addressing changing requirements elegantly. Say we wish to find issuers of the trades in addition to large trades (i.e., an IBM cancelled large trades), we simply add an additional filter without having to re-engineer the code, as shown below:

```
trades.stream()
  .filter(trade -> trade.getQuantity() > ONE_MILLION)
  .filter(Trade::isCancelledTrade)
  .filter(trade -> trade.getInstrument().equals("IBM"))
  .limit(10)
  .distinct()
  .forEach(System.out::println);
```

We can also add additional filters to the pipeline or other operations such as map, distinct or limit as shown in the above code.

Understanding Streams

A stream is a free flowing sequence of elements. Emails arriving in our inbox, alarms hitting the pilot's dashboard or health monitors ticking the heartbeats of a critically ill patient are all examples of sequences of various types of data elements, data flowing through continuously, incessantly.

Before Java 8, we did not have a capability of running through a list of elements and applying a set of functions to them elegantly (we could use for loops and if-else blocks, but not a great choice). Streams are very good at performing this task, applying various functions on the incoming data stream as the elements flow through. Streams do not hold any storage as that responsibility lies with collections.

> A stream is a continuous flow of elements upon which various data manipulation functions are applied

Streams Pipeline

Streams follow a pipeline architecture - a *pipes and filters* pattern. Every stream starts with a source of data, sets up a pipeline, processes the elements through a pipeline and finishes with a terminal operation. See the following picture that demonstrates this architecture pictorially:

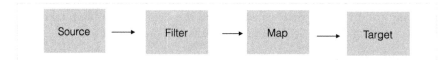

A pipeline is created with data events flowing through, with various intermediate operations being applied on individual events as they move through the pipeline. The stream is said to be terminated when the pipeline is disrupted with a terminal operation. An example of a terminal operation is to collect the aggregated sum to a list or may be printing out each of the filtered elements to a console etc.

Streams can be used in a parallel processing setup if it is required to use map-reduce process of computations. A new package java.util.stream was introduced in Java 8, with Stream as one of its core interface.

Sourcing Data

A source of a stream is nothing but a container of data, just like a simple flat file with few lines or a database table consisting of rows or an in-memory hash map with objects. More often than not, the source is most likely be a collection implementor. Streams do not hold any storage instead ask the source to provide the storage for streaming. The job of a stream is to *fetch* the data from a source, while source's job is to *hold* the data.

The streaming requirements dictate function(s) to be performed on the elements of the stream. These functions are filtering the elements into a basket (based on some conditions) or slicing the elements based on user-defined predicates or transforming the elements into other entities etc.

There are two different types of functions we can apply on a streaming data - an *intermediate* and *terminal* functions.

Intermediate Operations

As the name suggests, the intermediate operations are applied as an intermediate step in the pipeline. Operations such as filtering, mapping and transformation fall in this category. There can be many of such intermediate operations chained together one after the other, as shown in the picture below:

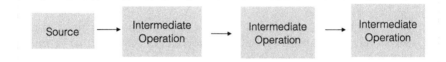

Notice, that the input to an intermediate operation or output from an intermediate operation is always a stream itself.

Terminal Operations

The terminal operation is the final operation that ends the pipeline (otherwise called a terminator). There's only one terminal operator on a stream which produces a definitive result (see the picture below) unlike an intermediate operation. Operations such as counting number of elements in a collection, collecting the elements into a list or simply printing the elements on a console all fall into terminal operations category.

Stream is expected to be immutable, any attempts to modify the collection will raise a `ConcurrentModifiedExcepti on` exception. The stream is exhausted once a terminal operation is used on it.

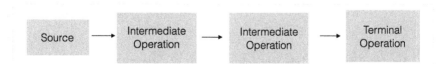

Streams Example

Consider an example of printing out a list of movies by reading them from a collection:

```
// DissectingStreams.java

// Our source of movies
List<Movie> movies =  ....;

private void findMoviesByDirector(String director) {
  movies
    .stream()
    .forEach(System.out::println);
}
```

What we have done is invoking a stream method on the Collection which retrieves the list of movies sequentially. On each of a movie, we applied a forEach operator which simply prints out movie detail. Here, the forEach is a terminal operator, meaning the pipeline ceases after the operation (hence called as a *terminator*). Once the stream is consumed, we cannot re-access it.

The above example has created a pipeline of source to target without any intermediate operation, hence no real data processing happening there. Let's add few intermediate operations to the pipeline.

Let's add a boolean function on the pipeline to check if the movies are directed by Steven Spielberg - a filter operator. The following snippet shows how we can add filters:

```
//DissectingStreams.java

// Our source of movies
List<Movie> movies =  ....;

private void findMoviesByDirector(String director) {
  movies.stream()
   .filter(m -> m.getDirector().equals(director))
   .forEach(System.out::println);
}
```

Executing the lambda will returns a list of Steven Spielberg movies. Using the filter, the program discards all those movies not directed by Spielberg. We can add as many filters as we wish to the pipeline. We can also add other intermediate operations such as map, as discussed next.

If we want to print only the movie's name and nothing else, we may need a function that extracts the movie name from the movie object (`movie.getName()`). This is exactly the feature of map intermediate operator. Here, the following code demonstrates the `map` function extracting the name of the movie given a movie object:

```
// DissectingStreams.java

movies
  .stream()
  .filter(m -> m.getDirector().equals(director))
  .map(Movie::getName)
  .forEach(System.out::println);
```

Each movie after successfully completing the filtering stage enters mapping stage. The `map` function gets the name of the movie by calling `getName` on the movie object and then gets printed out to the console. Note that we are using a method reference for fetching the name of the movie (you will learn about method and constructor references in due course).

Let's add one more operator to the pipeline - a `limit` operation. Limit operator cuts the output by a certain given number (in this case, we print three of Spielberg's movies due to limit clause):

```
// DissectingStreams.java

movies.stream()
  .filter(m -> m.getDirector().equals(director))
  .map(Movie::getName)
  .limit(3)
  .forEach(System.out::println);
```

As you have observed, the pipeline can be enhanced as you may wish based on slicing and dicing, transformation or reducing functionalities.

Summary

This chapter is a gentle introduction to streams. We learned the fundamentals of streams by working through basic features with examples backing up. We explored streams and non-streams strategies, understanding the intermediate and lazy operations.

11. WORKING WITH STREAMS

In this chapter, we will delve further into syntax and semantics of streams. We will look at creating streams, understanding the lazy and eager operations, exploring the key differences between collections and streams as well as finding out the streams that operate on primitive types.

Creating Streams

In our earlier examples, we mostly created streams from collections, such as movies or trades from an `ArrayList`. For example, `trades.stream()` or `movies.stream()` creates a stream from a collection as its datasource. However, streams can also be created from files or objects or even infinite data, not just collections. Let's run through various stream sources in the next section.

Empty Stream

An empty stream represents no values. There's a static method `empty` in the `Stream` interface to produce a stream of empty values, as the following code snippet demonstrates:

```
// CreatingStreams.java

private void emptyStreams() {
  Stream<Movie> emptyMoviesStream = Stream.empty();
  System.out.println("Movies: "+ emptyMoviesStream());
}
```

The return stream does not contains any data but behaves as a placeholder.

As expected, the size of an empty stream is equal to zero.

Values Stream

A stream can also be constructed using set of values. This is useful if our application needs initialising with static seed data. For example, the following examples creates a stream with movies populated in it.

```
// CreatingStreams.java

// Stream with initial values
Stream<String> movieNames =
  Stream.of("Gods Must Be Crazy",
            "Fiddler On The Roof",
            "Ben-Hur");
movieNames.forEach(System.out::println);
```

The static `Stream.of` method accepts a list of elements to create a stream with those elements. The method accepts variable arguments `vargs` as its parameter. There are two versions of the `of` method. One expects a list of values which we have already seen and the other that takes an input in a form of a single object such as an `Array` or `List`. See the code example below that demonstrates this version:

```
// CreatingStreams.java

//Array of strings
String[] movieNames = {"Gods Must Be Crazy","Fiddler On
The Roof","Ben-Hur"};

// Creating the stream with an array of strings
Stream<String> mNamesStream = Stream.of(movieNames);

//List of movies
List<String> moviesList = new ArrayList<>();
moviesList.add("The Sound of Music");
moviesList.add("Gone with the Wind");

// Creating the stream with a list of movies
Stream<List<String>> fromList = Stream.of(moviesList);
```

Here, the `Stream.of` method accepts a single argument (a `String[]` or `List<String>`) representing the movie names.

Collections Stream

We have learned how to create a stream from a collection in our introduction earlier on. Let's summarise this approach more formally here, if we have a data structure such as a List, Set or a Map, it can be turned to a stream by the application of the method stream on it.

In the following snippet the list of movies is turned to a stream by invoking the method stream (or parallelStream) on the collection.

```
// CreatingStreams.java

// Our list of movies
List<Movie> movies = ...;

// Stream from the list
Stream<Movie> movieStream = movies.stream();

// Or invoke parallelStream to run it in parallel mode
Stream<Movie> movieStream = movies.parallelStream();
```

The Collection interface has been enhanced with stream and parallelStream method, both being default methods, supporting data manipulations on collections.

Infinite Streams

An infinite stream, as the name indicates, produces a stream of elements incessantly. The stream is never exhausted and the elements pour out at a rate defined by the program. There are two variants in producing infinite streams - both discussed here under.

Using generate method

Stream API exposes a generate method for producing the infinite set of elements. Say, for example, we need to produce a list of random numbers, we can create a lambda expression as shown below:

```
// CreatingStreams.java

// Stream of random numbers
Stream<Double> randomGen =  Stream.generate(Math::random);

//Print the random number as they spit out
randomGen.forEach(s -> System.out.println(s));
```

When executed, the stream produces infinite random Doubles. The generate method accepts a Supplier (a Supplier accepts no arguments but returns set of data). Here the Math.random is the supplier producing ever flowing random Doubles. We can create our own Supplier that would create and supply the required data when asked for. Look at the following example where we create a supplier that generates random integers:

```
// CreatingStreams.java

Random rand = new Random();
// Create a supplier with the random generator
Supplier<Integer> randomIntegerSupplier = () -> {
  return rand.nextInt(100);
};

// Create a stream with supplier of random ints
Stream<Integer> randomIntStream = Stream
  .generate(randomIntegerSupplier);

randomIntStream.forEach(System.out::println);
```

Using *iterate* method

In our previous examples, we did not specify a start element when creating an infinite stream. If we wish to start the stream with a seed value, we can do so by using iterate method (rather than generate method). The iterate method accepts a function (UnaryOperator) and a seed value which is used by this function.

See the code below that produces a stream of whole numbers starting from 100:

```
// CreatingStreams.java

// Infinite stream of whole numbers.
Stream<Integer> intStream = Stream
  .iterate(100, n -> n+1);
```

Say we wish to create a sequence generator producing continuous identifiers starting from 1, we can do so using iterate function as shown below:

```
// Infinite stream of whole numbers starting from 1
Stream<Integer> wholeNumbers = Stream
  .iterate(1, i -> i + 1);

wholeNumbers.forEach(System.out::println);
```

File Streams

Similar to collections, we can have Files to stand in as a data source for a stream, reading out each line read from the file and streaming out. The

Files utility class has been retrofitted with the stream functionality by enhancing with a method called lines that produces a Stream<String> as output. This can be a very useful method for reading a file line by line, as demonstrated in the code below:

```
// CreatingStreams.java

// Create a Stream from a file
Stream<String> lines =
  Files.lines(Paths.get("/Users/mkonda/tmp.txt"));

// Process the stream
lines.forEach(System.out::println);
```

The Files class has another method called find which returns a stream of file paths (Stream<Path>), given a starting file or directory. See the code below:

```
// CreatingStreams.java

Path root = Paths.get("/Users/mkonda/Temp");
int maxDepth = Integer.MAX_VALUE;
BiPredicate<Path, BasicFileAttributes> filter = (path,
attrs) -> true;

// Create a Stream of Paths
Stream<Path> pathStream = Files.find(root, maxDepth,
filter);
pathStream.forEach(System.out::println);
```

Iteration Strategies

While previously we had to define the iteration explicitly, beginning with Java 8 we employ implicit internal iteration when working with streams. That is, we let the library take care of the iteration while we worry about the business logic.

Consider the following example that finds a list of classic movies using a for loop (traditional, explicit iteration approach):

```
// IterationStrategy.java

List<Movie> movies = MovieUtil.createMovies();

// External iteration (explicit declaration)
List<Movie> classics = new ArrayList<Movie>(10);
for(Movie m: movies){
  if(m.isClassic()){
    classics(m);
  }
}
```

Here, by creating the iteration explicitly, we control the flow by constructing an iterator, traversing through the elements and applying our business logic. If you carefully observe, the code is performing two functions - one is running through the list of elements and second is applying the filtering logic. This is something we have already talked earlier - the *how* and *what* parts. Browsing the collection is *how* part and applying the filtering logic is the *what* part. This might seem insignificant, especially as we were accustomed to that programming style, but combining the *how* and *what* functions leads to brittle code as well as inflexible design.

This is where the advantage of streams kicks in. Java designers cleverly wrapped up the *how* part underneath libraries automatically enabling the implicit iteration strategy. This let's us concentrate on the logic that needs to be applied rather than unnecessary iteration logic.

See the following code which uses no explicit iteration (the *how* part) but defines the application logic to be applied elegantly:

```
// IterationStrategy.java

// No more explicit iteration
movies.stream()
  .filter(Movie::isClassic)
  .map(Movie::getName)
  .forEach(System.out::println);
```

The invocation of the `stream` method is implicitly creating an iterator behind the scenes. Also notice that we did not create any intermediate storage variables as the underlying libraries deal with those low level requirements by default.

Lazy and Eager Streams

We learned that streams supports various functionalities such as filtering, mapping, collecting, limiting and so on. Although these functions looks plain and simple, they come also with a characteristic of either *laziness* or *eagerness.*

Any method that executes straight away is said to be as an eager method. The opposite of this is what defines the laziness. The lazy method will not be executed unless it's been explicitly asked to do so. Laziness will defer the execution on a pipeline until it finds a terminator (a terminal operation) at the end of the pipeline. Stream's pipeline of activities are clubbed together but muted until such time they are executed by an eager operation

Intermediate Operators are Lazy

Intermediate operations exhibit an important characteristic: laziness. We can associate numerous intermediate operations on a pipeline, all being in a dormant state waiting for someone to wake them up (a terminal operator brings them into action).

Suppose we create a method that applies some business logic on the movies stream:

```
// LazyAndEagerStreams.java

// The filter is never executed ..
  Stream<Movie> movieStream = movies
    .stream()
    .filter(m -> {
      System.out.println("Lazy operation");
      return m.isClassic();
    });

// ..unless we add a terminal operator(uncomment & rerun)
// movieStream.forEach(System.out::println);
```

In the above code segment, the filter method prints an info message before returning the boolean value. When you execute this lambda, the filter method will not be invoked and thus no print statements will get printed out on the console.

There is nothing wrong with this code. This behaviour is due to the characteristic of the filter operation, laziness. That is, filter is an intermediate operations and by design all intermediate operations are lazy. We can change this behaviour by adding a terminal operator such as count or collect to the pipeline. It's like getting into a swim lane for the race, awaiting for the signal to start the race. Unless the signal is out, race won't start.

We modify the code sample by associating a `count` or `limit` method to the pipeline:

```
// LazyAndEagerStreams.java

movies.stream()
  .filter( m ->{
    System.out.println("Lazy??");
    return m.isClassic();
  })
  .count();
  // or limiting
  //.limit(2);
}
```

The `count` (or `limit`) method immediately kickstarts the pipeline and we can see the print statements logged to the console instantly.

Along with filter, there are other methods such as `map`, `sorted`, `peek`, `distinct`, `limit` and `skip` which are lazy methods.

The end result of an intermediate operator is a stream itself. That is, filtering, mapping or limiting will produce another stream although the contents of the stream might be different. In fact, if an operation produces a stream as it's result, that operation is indeed an intermediate operation.

The output of an intermediate operation will always be a Stream. In fact, this is one of the ways to find if the operator is an intermediate one.

Terminal Operators are Eager

The terminal operators on the other hand return a value or `void`. Methods like `count`, `forEach`, `findFirst`, `findAny` or match methods like `allMatch`, `noneMatch` always execute the pipeline producing a result. The return result is the litmus test to check if the operator is in fact a terminator.

Let us consider the same example of filtering and mapping a movie stream. We define the filter and map operations with print statements and attaching a terminal operator `forEach` to the pipeline.

```
// LazyAndEagerStreams.java

movies.stream()
  .filter( m ->{
    System.out.println("Filtering");
    return m.isClassic();
  })
  .map(s->{
    System.out.println("Mapping");
    return s;
  })
  .forEach(System.out::println);
```

Until the forEach method is invoked on the movies stream, the pipeline will not be executed. Hence none of the print statements are written to console. This is because the forEach method is a terminal operator and all terminal operators's job is to kick start the pipeline and produce a final result.

See the output of the above program here once the forEach is attached to the pipeline:

```
Filtering // first movie is discarded
Filtering // second movie is a classic, sent to next stage
Mapping
Movie [name=Fiddler On The Roof]
Filtering // third movie is a classic too, so next stage
Mapping
Movie [name=Sound of Music]
Filtering // fourth movie is classic, on to next stage
Mapping
Movie [name=Ben-Hur]
Filtering // fifth movie is discarded
Filtering // sixth movie and so on..
..
```

Keep in mind that filtering block discards unsatisfied objects (non-classic movies) before sending it to the next stage. That is the reason why we see filtering being invoked on all the objects in the stream. Read the comments in the above example to understand the pipeline processing logic.

An intermediate operation on a stream is a lazy operation and always produces another stream instead of a result. The pipeline is muted until a terminal operator is attached to the end of the pipeline. The terminal operation is an eager method that always produces some value even if it means a void.

Streams And Collections

We learned that streams can be created from various data structures such as lists, maps, sets and others. On one level, both streams and collections may look the same and hence there's a chance we may be confused as to what the difference is.

Collections are used for storing elements ever since Java's inception. They provide functionalities such as insertion, removal and accessing of the elements in an efficient manner.

For example, look at Lists in Java. We use ArrayLists and LinkedLists to hold data for various purposes. But what makes the ArrayList our choice for a particular type of problem solving over LinkedList? If positional accessing of elements is our fundamental requirement, we choose ArrayList. But if speedy insertion and removal of data is the requirement, then we choose LinkedList dropping ArrayList altogether. Collections also have another contractual binding, that is, before an element is inserted into a collection, the element may have to be computed.

On the other hand, Streams are not concerned about storage requirements. They always depend on source data where the source can be a collection or a file etc. Without a datasource, there is little point of using streams.

Collections will always hold a finite amount of data due to the physical restrictions imposed by the JVM. While steams are free from storage restrictions, they can be designed to be infinite. For example, we can create infinite streams as we have explored earlier (by using generate or iterate functions). Lastly, the computation of elements is performed dynamically on the streaming data, more like on an on-demand basis.

Primitive Streams

At times, when working with streams, we wish to operate on primitive values like int, long, boolean or double rather than object references. For example, if we were to find out the aggregated quantity of all the trades, consider the following segment of code that uses no primitives:

```
//PrimitiveStreams.java

Optional<Integer> quantity = trades.stream()
  .map(Trade::getQuantity)
  .reduce(Integer::sum);

System.out.println(quantity);
```

We use `reduce` function in the above code. Reducing is an aggregation operation, a function that would accumulate the sum of all numbers to produce a final number.

As you can see from the above example, although the trade quantities are primitive `ints`, they are converted to `Integer` objects to aggregate them. The primitives are boxed up and returned as a result. Boxing (and unboxing) is an operation involved in conversion of primitive `int` to `Integer` class (or vice versa). The solution seems fine, but the issue is around the cost of boxing this block of code had to incur. Imagine, a huge datastore with primitives being converted to objects every time we start a calculation job. It is quite a poor strategy, indeed.

> The `Optional` is a new type introduced in Java 8 to combat null pointer issues. But remember it's not a magic bullet!

In order to mitigate this cost, Java 8 introduced streams for primitive values such as `ints`, `longs` and `doubles`. There are three specific stream implementations for supporting these primitives - `IntStream`, `LongStream` and `DoubleStream`.

Before we move on, notice the return type of the above `reduce` operation. The call is returning a new type called `Optional` type, which is a new type introduced in Java 8 for handling null pointer issues - more on this `Optional` type later.

IntStream

The `IntStream`, along with the other primitive streams (`LongStream`, `DoubleStream`) follows the same pattern. Let's run through some examples to understand them in detail.

We create an `IntStream` using a static method `of`, defined on the `IntStream` interface. Suppose we have an array of `ints`, it can be invoked to create an `IntStream` as shown below:

```
//PrimitiveStreams.java

// Array of integers
int[] ints = new int[]{10,20,30,40,50};

// Creating intstream from int array
IntStream intStream = IntStream.of(ints);
```

The array of ints is passed as an input to the static method of, which creates an IntStream in return.

The of method is overloaded, it can accept a list of integers, an array of ints or list of integers as vargs. See the second approach of passing vargs as the input to the method in the code below:

```
//PrimitiveStreams.java

// Creating the primitive stream from vargs
IntStream intStream = IntStream.of(1,2,3);
```

As we mentioned earlier, the primitive streams for double and longs follow the same principle. Let us write the code sample for DoubleStream below:

```
//PrimitiveStreams.java

double[] doubles = new double[]{4.2, 6.3, 8.5, 10.1};

// Using a single input object
DoubleStream doubleStream1 = DoubleStream.of(doubles);

// Using vargs type input
DoubleStream doubleStream2=DoubleStream.of(1.1,22.33);
```

Object Streams to Primitive Streams

We can also convert an object stream into a primitive streams using mapToInt method on the object stream.

For example, consider our earlier example of aggregating trade quality for a set of trades. We can use the mapToInt method which automatically converts the object stream to an IntStream which is a stream of primitive ints, as demonstrated below:

```
//PrimitiveStreams.java

// Boxed up stream
Stream<Integer> = trades.stream()
 .map(Trade::getQuantity);

// Object stream to a  primitive stream
IntStream quantityStream = trades
  .stream()
  .mapToInt(Trade::getQuantity);
```

The `mapToInt` accepts a `ToIntFunction` which is a specialization of a `Function` function producing primitive `int`s. We can take this one more step further by using `sum` method applied on the `IntStream` to get an aggregated result:

```
int quantity = trades.stream()
  .mapToInt(Trade::getQuantity)
  .sum();
```

As you can imagine, a `mapToDouble` and `mapToLong` functions also exists which are used to convert a normal (object) stream to a primitive `double` or primitive `long`. They expect a specialised function implementations of `ToDoubleFunction` or `ToLongFunction` to be passed to these methods.

Summary

In this chapter, we learned about creating various types of streams from a collection, a file, an array and others. We also looked at how to create infinite streams. We discussed the different iteration strategies especially understanding the implicit iteration defined by the streams behind the scenes. We also looked at the differences between collections and streams as well as understanding the characteristics of lazy and eager operations. Finally we have explored approaches of constructing streams for primitive values and converting from object to primitive streams.

12.STREAM OPERATIONS

Slicing and dicing data, aggregations and transformations, limiting, grouping and counting are some of the essential operations on streaming data. Java 8's streams support these functionality and solve them elegantly. We had a fore-taster of some of these functions such as `filter`, `map`, `count` and so on in earlier chapters, but we will dive deeper and explain how to use these functionalities here in this chapter. We will run through the common operations on streams using some basic examples in this chapter.

Filtering

The `filter` is an intermediate (hence lazy) operation, requiring a `Predicate` function as it's input parameter. Unless a terminal operator is attached to the pipeline, the `filter` operator won't be called. The filtering operation is a stateless intermediate operation. That is, the operation doesn't depend on the entire set of data but on it's own parameters.

Let's consider a simple example of creating a list of executives from our employees list. The `Employee` exposes a `isExecutive` method to check if the employee belongs to an executive category:

```
// StreamCommonOperations.java
Stream<Employee> employeeStream = employees
    .stream()
    .filter(Employee::isExecutive);
```

Here we are using the `filter` function to sieve through employees, list collecting only executives. The rest of the pipeline operations are invoked after filtering process is completed. As we chuck out the unwanted items in the beginning using the filtering operation, the executive list becomes quite manageable for further operations to be applied.

Chaining the *Filters*

We can create more feature rich (and complex) filters by *chaining* them to each other. Chaining allows reusing the existing filters rather than coding the whole logic in a new filter.

For example, in addition to finding executives, we may wish to check out the experience (seniority) of these executives. We drop in an another filter checking the seniority, as demonstrated in the following code:

```
// StreamCommonOperations.java

// Chaining the filters
Stream<Employee> employeeStream =
    employees.stream()
    .filter(Employee::isExecutive);
    .filter(Employee::isSenior)
```

As see in the above code, all executives are gathered and passed through another test to check if they have senior level experience using second filter. We can add as many filters as we wish, for example, the following code attaches another filter to the pipeline checking if the executives belong to Marketing department:

```
// StreamCommonOperations.java

Stream<Employee> employeeStream =
    employees.stream()
    .filter(Employee::isSenior)
    .filter(Employee::isExecutive);
    .filter(e -> e.getDepartment().equals("Marketing"))
```

Mapping

Mapping is an essential function to transform data. It is an intermediate , lazy and stateless operation which applies a function to an input producing the desired result. For example, extracting an employee given her employee id or fetching the movie actors from a movie.

As we already seen in earlier chapters, mapping is carried out by invoking the `map` method on the stream. The `map` method accepts a standard `Function` function, where the `Function` accepts a value and produces a result in return.

For example, to find employee's names from a list of employees, we create a function that accepts an employee and outputs a name. Consider the following code:

```
// StreamCommonOperations.java

Stream<String> employeeStream = employees
   .stream()
   .map(Employee::getName);
```

The `getName` function will be applied to every `Employee` element flowing through the stream to obtain `Employee`'s name. In other words, the input to the `map` function is an `Employee` (the sequence of elements flowing through the pipeline are `Employee` objects), while the output from the `map` function is a `String`. Thus converting `Employee` object to a `String` is the job of a mapper.

Chaining the Mappers

We can also chain the mappers, similar to chaining the filters. Say we want the employee names be changed to upper case after pulling them out from the employees list:

```
// StreamCommonOperations.java

Stream<String> employeeStream = employees
   .stream()
   .map(Employee::getName)
   .map(String::toUpperCase);
```

Similar to filtering, the mapping operation is stateless operation. That is, it solely works on the data that's been given as it's argument. Also, note that it is a lazy operation too.

> Filtering and mapping are stateless, intermediate operations.

Flat Map

At times, we wish to present the output as a flattened list rather than a list of lists. For example, in the movie example below, we are fetching a stream of list of actors (Stream<List<Actors>>):

```
// StreamCommonOperations.java

Stream<List<Actor>> actorsListStream = movies
    .stream()
    .map(Movie::getActors);

actorsListStream.forEach(System.out::println);

//Output (prints as two lists for two given movies):
[Julie Andrews, Christopher Plummer]
[Sam Neil, Jeff Goldblum]
```

The output of this program will result in a *stream of list of actors* as oppose to stream of actors. In order to get to the actors, we subsequently need to create a stream (another one!) from the list of actors (remember, collections are one of the datasources for a stream). That is, we are looking at stream of streams! Ideally we wish to have a flattened output of list of actors from different movies, irrespective of the inputs being used. For this to happen, we need to flatten the list and the flatMap is the function that's been used to obtain the result:

```
// StreamCommonOperations.java

// Stream of Actors not Stream of List of Actors!
Stream<Actor> actorsStream = movies
    .stream()
    .flatMap(m -> m.getActors().stream());

actorsStream.forEach(System.out::println);
```

We invoke flatMap on the stream passing the lambda expression of extracting the actors. In turn need to invoke the stream method on the lambda expression that returns a list. This way, the output is flattened and we simply receive a stream of actors instead stream of list of actors.

Collecting

The elements can be collected into a collection by invoking the collect method on the stream. There are two versions of collecting process: a simple version which we will look here, also an advanced version that requires customisation, which is covered in the next chapter.

The collect method is used to gather the elements to a collection such as a list, set or a map. It accepts an instance of a Collector, which is a mechanism for collecting that accumulates the inputs into a collection. It is is a new interface introduced in Java 8, a concrete implementation of this interface is expected by the `collect` method. Writing a concrete implementation is however a tricky job, hence we discuss this approach in next chapter. Fortunately the Java library has an utility class called `Collectors` (note that it is a plural name) that implements this `Collector` interface. We simply use the utility methods provided by this class to collect the inputs into a collection. Let's run through various implementations that we can use to collect the data using the off-the-shelf `Collectors` methods.

Collecting to a List

If we wish to collect the stream of data into an `ArrayList`, perhaps a set of big trades, we simply use the `Collectors.toList()` method, as shown below:

```java
// StreamCommonOperations.java

List<Trade> bigTrades = trades
  .stream()
  .filter(Trade::isBigTrade)
  .collect(Collectors.toList());

bigTrades.forEach(System.out::println);
```

As shown above, all the trades that passed the big-trade filter condition are collected into an `ArrayList`. The return type (`List<Trade>`) indicates that we have collected the big trades successfully to a list.

As the `toList()` is a static method, we can import the method using the `static` import facility, which makes the code shorter and more readable:

```java
// StreamCommonOperations.java

// Static importing toList method
import static java.util.stream.Collectors.toList;

// use toList which expresses the intent
Collection<Trade> tradesList = trades
  .stream()
  .collect(toList());
```

Collecting to a Set

Instead of collecting to a list, if our requirement dictates gathering elements into a `Set`, we use `Collectors.toSet()` method to collect the elements into a `Set`. This is demonstrated in the following code segment:

```
// StreamCommonOperations.java

Set<Trade> bigTrades = trades
  .stream()
  .filter(Trade::isBigTrade)
  .collect(toSet());

bigTrades.forEach(System.out::println);
```

The `toSet` method is imported as a `static` method on the class.

Collecting to a Map

Additionally, there is a `toMap` method which collects the elements into a name-value paired map. The `toMap` method accepts two `Functions` as arguments: one for creating the key and the other for the creation of the value.

Suppose, we wish to create a `Map` with the *name* of the movie as the key and actors as the *value*. The following segment shows how we can create and populate a key-value `Map`:

```
// StreamCommonOperations.java#collectingToAMap

// The key-values are supplied by two functions
Map<String, List<Actor>> movieActorsMap = movies
  .stream()
  .collect(toMap(Movie::getName,
                 movie -> movie.getActors()));

// Print them out to the console
movieActorsMap.forEach(
  (name, actors) -> System.out.println(name+actors)
);

//Output as key-value pairs
Jurassic Park[Sam Neil, Jeff Goldblum]
Sound Of Music[Julie Andrews, Christopher Plummer]
```

The first argument (getName) fetches the name of the movie forming the key to the map, while the second argument invokes `getActors` on the movie to fetch the cast of that movie forming the value of the map.

Distinct, Limit and Skip

In data manipulating exercises, removing duplicates, limiting the output to a pre-specified count and skipping the unwanted elements are some of the essential operations expected to be part of the framework. Streams provides the `distinct,` `limit` and `skip` functionality for this purpose.

Distinct function

Distinct operation is used to remove duplicates from the data set. For example, if we want to pick the distinct employees from a list that may have duplicate entires, we use the `distinct` operation. See the `distinct` function in action below:

```
// StreamCommonOperations.java#distinctEmployees

// Removing duplicate entries from the list
Stream<String> employeeStream = employees
   .stream()
   .map(Employee::getName)
   .distinct();
```

The return value of a `distinct` method is a Stream, making it an intermediate lazy operation. However, keep in mind that distinct is a stateful operator. Unlike `filter` and `map`, it needs to have a knowledge about the whole set of data to remove the duplicates.

Limit Operation

Limiting output is a top requirement when working with data. Instead of sending reams of data to the client, we may need to limit it to the first hundred or top ten elements, for example. This is where the `limit` operation comes handy. It accepts an integer as it's input parameter, which represents the number of the elements the output is limited to. For example, the following code shows that we are only interested in the first three employees:

```
// StreamCommonOperations.java#limitOutput

Stream<String> employeeStream = employees
   .stream()
   .map(Employee::getName)
   .limit(3);
```

The limit operation is useful when our pipeline operations are producing lot of data and we wish to provide the only *n* number of elements. If the code is parallelly run, limit operation will produce the result based on encounter order of the elements. Note that the performance of the limit operation depends on the ordering of the stream. If the ordering of the stream is important, it would be wise to switch to a sequential mode (by invoking sequential method on the stream). Otherwise, if ordering is the least priority, parallel runs may be preferred.

Skip Operation

While limit chops off the remaining data set after the specified count, the skip operation is opposite. That is, the skip operation *skips* elements before producing the output.

For example, we can skip first two elements in the employee stream by simply invoking the skip method passing in a value (value 2 in this case as we wish to skip first two elements) . The skip method accepts an integer as it's parameter representing the number of elements to be skipped. The code below demonstrates skipping function in action:

```
// StreamCommonOperations.java#skipEmployees

// Skip processing the first three elements.
Stream<String> employeesNamesStream = employees
  .stream()
  .skip(3)
  .map(Employee::getName);
```

If the size parameter greater than actual stream size (meaning we are expected to skip the whole list!), an empty stream will be returned. For example, skipping 10 elements when we have a set of five elements will return an empty stream.

Short Circuit Operations

Java 8 provides search and find functionalities on streaming data using finder and match methods. These handful methods are designed to match and find the elements from a data set. These methods are also called as short circuit operations because the pipeline processing will cease executing once the element in question is found. Hence, short circuit operations carry a great performance benefit because they don't have to sieve through the entire population.

Let's look at some examples of find and match functions.

Find Methods

Find methods such as `findAny` and `findFirst` finds the element based on some conditions. For example, `findAny` will search for *any* element that matches the condition while `findFirst` returns the first element from the list that matches the condition.

findFirst method

The `findFirst` method is used to fetch the *first* element that meets the condition from the entire set. For example, say we want to find *any one large trade* from list of trades population. We are after the first large trade rather than sieving through all large trades. It is very clear that once the filtering logic is executed, we return the element (this element is indeed the first element) and pipeline should cease to execute. We use the `findFirst` method to satisfy this requirement, as shown in the following code snippet:

```
// StreamOperations.java#findFirst

// Fetching the first big trade
Optional<Trade> firstBigTrade = trades
   .stream()
   .filter(Trade::isBigTrade)
   .findFirst();

System.out.println(firstBigTrade.get());
```

The `filter` function retrieves the large trade when the big-trade-condition is met. Then the `findFirst` will come into action to return this large trade, stopping the pipeline execution instantly.

There's a chance that the `findFirst` might not yield any results in which case a null pointer reference may bubble up. To avoid nasty null pointer exceptions, `findFirst` returns an `Optional` which acts as a safety guard against null pointers. We will learn about `Optional` types in the next few sections.

findAny method

Instead of finding the *first* of the large trades, if we want to find *any* of the big trades from the stream, we use `findAny` function instead:

```
// StreamCommonOperations.java#findAny

// Finding any of the big trade
Optional<Trade> anyTrade = trades
  .stream()
  .filter(t -> t.isBigTrade())
  .findAny();
```

You may have noticed the similarity in `findFirst` and `findAny` methods. Well, they are pretty much the same except they behave different when are executed in parallel mode. The `findAny` will return any trade that satisfies the condition *instantly* and aborts the rest of the code execution. Where as, the `findFirst` will have to wait until all the data is returned before checking for the first available result that satisfies the requirement.

If our code is parallel-ready, then we should ideally use the `findAny` method so we know the result will be obtained instantly when the condition is met without having to wait for processing the rest of the elements. If the code is designed for a single-thread execution, then `findFirst` is the best choice.

Match Methods

The second category of matching methods, `anyMatch`, `allMatch`, `noneMatch`, are used to check the elements against a predicate, hence returning a boolean value of `true` or `false` (as oppose to an object returned by the *find* methods). The `anyMatch`, `allMatch` and `noneMatch` methods accepts a `Predicate` for conditional checking.

anyMatch method

The `anyMatch` is used to check if an element satisfies the given `Predicate` expression. Say, if we wish to check if the list of trades has a cancelled trade, we use `anyMatch` as shown here:

```
// StreamCommonOperations.java#anyMatch

boolean cancelledTrade = trades
  .stream()
  .anyMatch(t -> t.getStatus().equals("CANCELLED"));
```

Here, we run through the list of trades, checking each trade's status. If the status matches the given predicate, the pipeline execution terminates immediately returning true value.

allMatch method

Suppose we wish to find if *all* trades match a certain criteria, in that case we use `allMatch` method. For example, if we want to check if all our trades are against IBM, we design the program as shown below:

```
// StreamCommonOperations.java#allMatch

boolean ibmTrades = trades
    .stream()
    .allMatch(t -> t. getInstrument().equals("IBM"));
```

This code checks if all trades are IBM trades and if each and every trade is an IBM trade, the function will return true.

noneMatch method

Say, we like to find out if none of the trade is cancelled, how do we do that? We can use `noneMatch` function by passing a `Predicate` that evaluates the condition:

```
// StreamCommonOperations.java#noneMatch

boolean cancelledTrade = trades
    .stream()
    .noneMatch(Trade::isCancelledTrade);
```

The cancelled trade predicate checks for the cancelled trades and returns true if none of the trades are cancelled.

Reducing

Reducing is a way of aggregating to a single result, like aggregating the total movie collections over a week or finding out the average age of a child in an exam held countrywide and so on. Streams support reduction operations by providing a `reduce` method. This method, as expects, aggregates a set of values producing a single value.

The `reduce` operation accepts a single argument of type `BinaryOperator`. Remember, `BinaryOperator` is a specialised `BiFunction` that consumes two operands of same type returning a result of the same type.

Suppose we wish to aggregate the sum value of the quantity of all the trades given. We can extract the quantity of each trade and provide it to reduce function so it can accumulate the value. See this in action in the code example given below:

```
// StreamCommonOperations.java#reducingTradeQuantity

Optional<Integer> totalQuantity = trades
  .stream()
  .map(Trade::getQuantity)
  .reduce((a,b) -> a+b);

System.out.println("Agg quantity: "+totalQuantity.get());
```

The reduction operation is passed in with a lambda expression (that implements a `BinaryOperator`) which simply adds the first value to the second value. The way the reduce function works is not complex but understanding the function is advisable.

Here in our example, the first element, a, in the above expression, is the seed or initial element. However, we did not define the initial element and hence it is empty. The empty first element is then added to the second input, represented by b. The elements are accumulated when flown through the reduction function. The accumulated value becomes the initial element (a) in the next iteration while the next quantity fetched from the stream becomes the second element (b). This process of accumulation continues until the stream is exhausted and the final result returned back to the user.

The return value is interesting to note. It is of an `Optional` type for handling null pointers just in case.

The same example can be re-written using primitive stream version (thus avoiding boxing operation):

```
//StreamCommonOperations.java#reducingPrimitiveVersion

OptionalInt totalQuantity = trades
  .stream()
  .mapToInt(Trade::getQuantity)
  .reduce(Integer::sum);

System.out.println("Total quantity (unboxed version):
"+totalQuantity.getAsInt());
```

We use `mapToInt` method so the quantity is expressed as primitive int (not converted to `Integer`) before feeding it to reduction operation. The reduction function is accumulates the inputs, this time using a static method sum on the `Integer` class.

Consider another example, this time creating a string of all instruments extracted from the trades list. The instruments are expected to be returned as a comma separated String.

```
// StreamCommonOperations.java#reduceNoSeed

// Using reduce function
Optional<String> instList = trades
  .stream()
  .map(Trade::getInstrument)
  .reduce((a,b)-> a+","+b);

System.out.println("Comma separated instruments:
"+instList);
```

As shown in the above example, we are fetching instrument of each trade using map function, then feeding it to the next stage of reduction. A BinaryOperator function is defined to join up the given inputs with a comma delimiter. The function is then applied to the inputs using reduce function which simply uses the BinaryOperator to do the job.

reduce with seed value

In our earlier example, we did not supply any initial or seed value. There's an overloaded method of reduce function that accepts a seed value and an accumulator function. See the following segment of code that sums up list of numbers with a seed value given as the input along with the lambda that aggregates these numbers (an accumulator):

```
// StreamCommonOperations.java#reduceUsingSeed

List<Integer> numberStream=Arrays.asList(11, 13, 12, 15);
int SEED_VALUE = 100;

int result = numberStream
  .stream()
  .reduce(SEED_VALUE, (i, j) -> i + j);
```

Note that the return time is not of an Optional type this time. The reason is that when we provide an initial value to the accumulator function and hence we are expected to receive a final definitive outcome.

We have seen the Optional type popping up few times in our examples, may be it is a good time to talk about the Optional type here.

127

Optional **Type**

No doubt we all have been through the perils of null pointer exceptions in Java. The null pointer exception is as famous as the English weather. The good news is a new type called Optional was introduced in Java 8 to save us from the null pointer issues graciously.

When working with objects, there is always a possibility that the objects may not have been created. When we dereference these objects that weren't created as yet, a null pointer exception will be thrown. Ideally code should handle the null pointer cases but it is cumbersome to do such validations as there are various marginal cases that may slip the net.

The Optional type is simply a container with a value - value can either be a null or non-null value. The trick is how we access that value. Optional provides isPresent method that will return true if it (container) has a non-null value or false otherwise. If the isPresent returns true, we can use a get method on the Optional reference to fetch the non-null value.

For example, we wish to aggregate the number of attendees attending various talks at a conference on a daily basis. We know that the reduce function returns an aggregated result enclosed in an Optional. The following example demonstrates this point:

```
// OptionalType#sumOfAttendees

// List of attendees to various talks
List<Integer> attendees = Arrays.asList(22, 10, 13, 9);

// Total attendees at the conference
Optional<Integer> totalAttendees = attendees
  .stream()
  .reduce(Integer::sum);

// Using isPresent on the optional to fetch result
int total =
  totalAttendees.isPresent()?totalAttendees.get():0;

System.out.println("Total attendees: "+total);
```

The return values of the reduction is an Optional which has a get method to fetch the value. However, before you get the value, there's a check you should ideally perform by invoking isPresent method.

The isPresent method is an indicator if the result value exists in the Optional container. If the method returns true indicating the presence

128

of a value, we can then proceed to the next step of fetching the value using the get method. If we don't use the isPresent function, we may end up in the same sticky situation as previously we had with the null pointer. In the code example above, we invoke the isPresent on the Optional to return a final value. As the ternary operator suggests, if there's a value in the container, go get it else simply return zero as the return result (thus avoiding the null pointer).

Let's find out what happens if we access the Optional which has a null value. This is shown in the following example:

```
// OptionalType.java#noAttendeesOptional

// No attendees to the conference!
List<Integer> attendees = Arrays.asList();

// This should have no value as there are no attendees
Optional<Integer> noAttendees attendees
  .stream()
  .reduce(Integer::sum);

// Access the optional (not the right way)
System.out.println(noAttendees.get());
```

We aggregated the sum of all the attendees to the conference, in this case, a null value should be present in the Optional result. However, invoking the Optional null-value using get method without using isPresent method will definitely result in an exception. Running the code above results in an exception as shown below:

```
Exception in thread "main"
java.util.NoSuchElementException: No value present
  at java.util.Optional.get(Optional.java:135)
  . .
```

Hence, to avoid this embarrassment, we modify the access to the optional using isPresent:

```
// OptionalType.java #noAttendeesOptional
. . . .
// Access the optional (the right way!)
if (noAttendees.isPresent())
  System.out.println(noAttendees.get());
```

Creating *Optional* Types

We can create an instance of an `Optional` using static method `of` as shown in the following `Student` example:

```
// OptionalType.java#creatingOptional

// Create an Optional instance
Student student = new Student();
Optional<Student> studentOptional = Optional.of(student);

// and access it
studentOptional.ifPresent(System.out::println);
```

In the above code, what if the student instance is `null`? If we try to access the value via `Optional`, we may get a null pointer as we are not using the `Optional` in the correct sense. In such situations, `ofNullable` is used.

ofNullable Optional

The `ofNullable` static method on `Optional` is a handy method to rescue us from situations where the null value cannot be ruled out. Employing the `ofNullable` would either return an `Optional` with the non-null value wrapped up or an empty `Optional`. This avoids a null reference being thrown when accessed by the program. See the example code below where we use the `ofNullable` if the student instance is null.

```
// OptionalType.java#creatingOptional (contd)

// Deliberately set the student instance to null
Student student = null;
Optional<Student> studentOptional = Optional
 .ofNullable(student);
```

Keep in mind, creating an instance of a student (`Student student = new Student`) is different to setting a null value (`Student student = null`) to the `Student`. In the former case, the instance exists where as in the later case the instance has not been created and hence when we dereference it, a null pointer is inevitable.

ifPresent method

There is another handy method called `ifPresent` on the `Optional` which accepts a `Consumer` function to work with a non-null value. That is, the `Consumer` comes into action if there's a non-null optional value else it does nothing. For example,

```
// OptionalType.java#usingIfPresent

Student student = new Student();
// student reference is valid
Optional<Student> studentOptional = Optional.of(student);

// ifPresent accepts a Consumer - printing in this case
studentOptional.ifPresent(System.out::println);
```

The `ifPresent` invocation prints the value if the optional has a value in the first place, else nothing gets printed out. Keep in mind, a null pointer is thrown is the value is null.

Don't expect `Optional` solve your `NullPointerException` headaches!

orElse *method*

Finally if there is any chance that an object can be null in some obscure circumstances, we can define a default implementation to avoid the null pointer. In this instance, we use `orElse` method to plug in a default implementation.

As shown in the following example, we use the default student using the `orElse` method if the `student` optional is null. This way, if the actual value doesn't exist we can replace with an alternative default value.

```
// OptionalType.java#usingOrElse

// Two students - one null and other is default student
Student student = null;
Student defaultStudent = new Student();
defaultStudent.setName("Default John");

Optional<Student> optionalStudent =
  Optional.ofNullable(student);

// Accessing the above will throw a NoSuchElementException
// System.out.println(studentOptional.get());

// In this case, use orElse to fetch a default value
String name =
  optionalStudent.orElse(defaultStudent).getName();
```

Should we wish to throw an exception if we are expecting a null reference to the optional, then `orElseThrow` method is what we should invoke:

```
// OptionalType.java#usingOrElseThrow

Optional<Student> studentOptional = null;

// Exception will be thrown as studentOptional is null
studentOptional.orElseThrow(Exception::new);
```

This is a neat way of creating an exception and throwing it back to the client should the `Optional` object doesn't contain any value.

`Optional` Filtering and Mapping

We can also add filtering and mapping functions on the `Optionals`. The filter on an `Optional` expects a `Predicate` that returns an `Optional` as the return. For example, we want to find out if a teacher has been allocated to a student, the following code demonstrates this:

```
// OptionalType.java#filteringAndMapping

Student s = new Student();
s.setName("John Lingham");
s.setTeacher(new Teacher());

studentOptional
    .filter(student -> student.hasTeacher())
    .ifPresent(System.out::println);

//Output
Student [name=John Lingham, teacher=Teacher [name=Prof.
Pandit]]
```

Similarly, we can transform the `Optional` to another form (fetching a student's name rather than the full student details), using map function on the `Optional`:

```
// OptionalType.java#filteringAndMapping

studentOptional
    .map(student -> student.getName())
    .ifPresent(System.out::println);
```

The name of the student is extracted out from the `Optional` object, given student.

132

Summary

In this chapter, we learned about various functions for slicing, aggregation and transformation of data using filters and mappers as well as operations that support limiting, skipping and distinct features on data. We also worked with reduction, find and match functions. We finally learned `Optional` type used for handling null pointers.

13. ADVANCED STREAMS

Grouping and partitioning of data is a fundamental requirement when working with data sets. We work with them in real life everyday too, for example, we group movies baed on genres, we develop set of bad credits, we mimic global climate patterns and so on. In this, we will walk through the grouping and partitioning functions in detail.

Grouping

You may have worked on segregating data using *group by* clauses when working on databases using SQL. Java provides similar function called `groupingBy` for categorising the elements. The `stream.collect` method expects this `groupingBy` function.

However, as we did in earlier chapters, we use the `Collectors` utility class to invoke the `groupingBy` method (similar to `Collectors.toList` or `toSet`) than providing a Collector of our own.

Java 8 provides `groupingBy` function similar to SQL's grouping clause

---

The grouping feature is a *name-values* pairing type operation accepting a `Function`. For each group, there's always a key as well as set of values against that key. For example, *classics* movies group will have classics as the key and possibly Wizard of Oz, Singing in the Rain, Sound of Music etc as group's values. The data structure we use to represent this kind of classification is a `Map` container.

Say, we have a requirement to categorise list of employees into departments.

We use `groupingBy` method to do such segregation. We can say the department will be the key while employees under each department would become the values.

The `groupingBy` method has two variants: one that accepts a `Function` type as its input parameter, and the other which will take in another `Collector` along with the `Function`. The second variant helps us achieve multi-level grouping which is discussed further down.

Single-level Grouping

Consider the following snippet that collects the employees from a stream and groups them according to a department function.

```
// GroupingAndPartitioning.java#groupingByDepartment

// Department is the key, employees are values
Map<String, List<Employee>> deptEmployees  = employees
  .stream()
  .collect(Collectors.groupingBy(e -> e.getDepartment()));
```

Here, we are providing a lambda expression of type `Function` to the `groupingBy` method. As mentioned earlier, the output of a groupingBy function is a map, which represents name-value paired container. The lambda expression extracts the department which becomes the key of the map container while the employees that satisfy the grouping condition will be the values. The return type of `Map<String, List<Employee>>` indicates this.

When you execute the above program, we will see the output printed to the console as shown below:

```
// GroupingAndPartitioning.java#groupingByDepartment

//Employees grouped by department
{
  Finance=[Employee1, Employee2],
  Strategy=[Employee1,Employee3, Employee 9]
}
```

The above output shows that each employee is *grouped* under a department.

Grouping conditions can be changed easily by modified lambda expression, for example, the following snippet demonstrates the grouping of employees by city:

```
// GroupingAndPartitioning.java#groupByCity
// Employees grouped by city
Map<String, List<Employee>> cityEmployees = employees
   .stream()
   .collect(groupingBy(Employee::getCity));

// Output
{New York=[Employee 1, Employee 4], London=[Employee 2,
Employee 5], Hyderabad=[Employee 3]}
```

Multilevel Grouping

Multilevel grouping is a useful feature if we have a requirement to group a certain set of values in two or more levels. For example, grouping employees by department living in a city, or preparing a list of classic movies falling under thriller genre, etc.

We can satisfy this requirement using the second variant of groupingBy method which accepts a Function and another Collector as its inputs. That means, as a second parameter, we can provide another groupingBy (which returns Collector implementation).

Consider the following code segment which retrieves employees based on a department and living in a city using a multi-level grouping feature:

```
// GroupingAndPartitioning.java#groupingByDeptAndCity

Map<String,Map<String,List<Employee>>> deptAndCityEmp =
   employees
   .stream()
   .collect(groupingBy(
      (Employee::getDepartment),
      groupingBy(Employee::getCity))
   );

// Output
{
 Finance={London=[Employee 2]},
 Marketing={New York=[Employee 1, Employee 2],
}
```

Let us dissect this code example. The groupingBy is accepting two parameters (the second variant): a department and another groupingBy function. The department acts as a key while the values are fed from the second groupingBy function. Here's where the groupingBy turns interesting. The second groupingBy allocates city as the key and employees

136

that fit the bill as values. So, for each department, we group employees in various cities, as shown in the output above.

The return result is worth having a look. We have a *map of map* of groups! That is, employees grouped by department and then again grouped by city.

We can take this even further. We can create nested grouping, grouping in grouping without any limit. This is a powerful way of making *n-dimensional* grids, nesting the multi-level group clauses to each other. For example, if we like to group employees by department and by city and by executives and by region, we can simply nest the groupingBy methods. I will let you venture this exercise by yourself.

> We can create n-dimensional grids by nesting multi-level groupingBy functions.

A special case of grouping is to partition the data in two splits, which is the subject of the next section.

Partitioning

We usually wish to split a class of children into boys and girls, a list of employees into executives and non-executives, or splitting programmers into Java and C# skills etc. Here we are *partitioning* a set of data into *two* individual categories based on a predicate. Unlike in grouping, the data is split into only two categories - based on true or false key in partitioning.

Similar to groupingBy, the collect method on the Stream accepts a partitioning function, an implementation of Collector interface. Following the same pattern we have used in grouping feature, we take the assistance of the utility class Collectors's partitioningBy method to return a Collector.

Consider an example of partitioning the data based on executive role. The partitioningBy method accepts a Predicate to check if the given employee is an executive. The key can always be one of the true or false values, hence the Map will always have Boolean as it's key. For instance, if we wish to partition our employees based on executives vs non-executives, we write our program as demonstrated here below:

```
//GroupingAndPartitioning.java#partitionByExecutives

// categorised by exec and non-execs
Map<Boolean, List<Employee>> execEmployees = employees
    .stream()
    .collect(partitioningBy(Employee::isExecutive));

// Output: true are execs, false are non-execs
true: [Employee 0, Employee 99]]
false: [Employee 1, Employee 2, Employee 3]
```

The employees are split into two groups - one group based on `true` value (i.e., executives) and other on `false` (i.e., non-executives).

PartitioningBy accepting a collector

Moving on, there's a second variant of `partitioningBy` method: method taking in a `Collector` (in addition to a `Predicate`). That means, we can partition the data and then *group* according to the given condition.

Let's suppose we were asked to group the exec and non-exec employees according to their department. We would be doing two things here: partitioning based on the employees rank (exec/non-exec) *and* group them according to their department. This is demonstrated in the following code example:

```
//GroupingAndPartitioning.java#partitioningAndGrouping

Map<Boolean,  Map<String,List<Employee>>>  execEmployees  =
employees
    .stream()
    .collect(partitioningBy((Employee::isExecutive),
            groupingBy(Employee::getDepartment)));

// Output
// Partitioned by exec/non-exec and then grouped by dept
false:{IT=[Employee 1], Marketing=[Employee3,Employee4]}
true:{Finance=[Employee5],Strategy=[Employee3}
```

The `partitioningBy` method accepts a `Predicate` as well as a `groupingBy` function. The output shows two groups - execs and non-execs derived by using partitioning function, followed by employees grouped based on their department.

Multilevel Partitioning

Just as we learned about multi-level grouping, we can also create multilevel partitioning too. Multilevel partitioning is the partitioning on the partitioned data. For example execs and non-execs partitioned further by seniority:

```
// GroupingAndPartitioning.java#multilevelPartitioning

Map<Boolean, Map<Boolean,List<Employee>>> execEmployees =
employees
  .stream()
  .collect(partitioningBy((Employee::isExecutive),
          partitioningBy(Employee::isSenior)));

// Output
false:{false=[Employee 1], true=[Employee 3, Employee 3]}
true:{false=[], true=[Employee 0, Employee 2, Employee 3]}
```

Notice the returned types of the function. It is a map of a maps both having boolean keys. That is, we always expect true or false classified data sets when working with partitioning functions.

Custom Collectors

We learned that the `collect` method on the stream accepts an implementation of `Collector` interface. So far, we have taken the assistance of the `Collectors` class which provided default collection algorithms such as `toList`, `groupingBy`, `partitioningBy` etc.

In addition to the above library functions, we can also implement our own collector if a special requirement arises - may be a collector to store the trades in a specialized trade container.

The `collect` method accepts an implementation of `Collector`. A `Collectors` utility class provides pre-built `Collector` implementations.

Let's look at the `Collector` interface we have been talking about for a while.

`Collector` Interface

The fundamental aim of a `Collector` interface is accumulating the input elements, reducing (aggregating) the output and finally storing the result to a container. The enrichment or transformation operations can also be applied on the data while processing is in progress. The reduction operation is designed to be run sequential or parallel mode, suiting our program requirements.

The `Collector` interface definition is provided below:

```
public interface Collector<T, A, R> {
  Supplier<A> supplier();
  BiConsumer<A, T> accumulator();
  BinaryOperator<A> combiner();
  Function<A, R> finisher();
  Set<Characteristics> characteristics();
  ....
}
```

The collector interface has five methods, all working together to produce the desired functionality. Understanding and working through them is a bit involved, so let's get a handle on them.

- **Accumulator**: The accumulator is a user defined lambda expression accumulating the data to reduce to a final value before inserting into the container.
- **Supplier**: The supplier is a function that creates a suitable container for application's requirement. For example, should we wish to create a custom container for holding comma delimited data, we can ask the `Supplier` to provide a container of `StringBuilder` type with comma delimiters appended.
- **Combiner**: The combiner is an aggregator where it combines or merges two intermediate results to produce a final result. It works on two incomplete results to produce a result, returning it to the caller.
- **Finisher**: The finisher is a transformation function to be applied on the elements transforming them from type A to type B.
- **Characteristics**: The characteristics are properties for defining the reduction implementations. These characteristics are defined as enum properties.

The `Collector` interface also declares a static method named `of` for creating a `Collector` by accepting the above classes (that is, accumulator, supplier, etc.)

Checkout the interface definition here below:

```
// Collector interface defintion

static<T,R> Collector<T,R,R> of(Supplier<R> supplier,
BiConsumer<R,T> accumulator,BinaryOperator<R> combiner,
Characteristics... characteristics) {
  .. ..
}
```

There is also an overloaded method which accepts the above four classes
and a Function called finisher:

```
static<T,R> Collector<T,R,R> of(Supplier<R> supplier,
BiConsumer<R,T> accumulator,BinaryOperator<R> combiner,
Function<A,R> finisher,Characteristics… characteristics) {
  .. ..
}
```

Custom Collector

The easy place to start creating our own collector would be the stream's
collect method which accepts three arguments: the supplier, accumulator
and combiner. The characteristics are either derived or defaulted.

Suppose we want to create a string of all instruments for a given set of
trades. First we need a supplier (container) to hold our result. The
StringBuilder will serve our purpose as we are simply creating and
appending strings.

The following code will demonstrate this, i.e, creating a supplier (all the
snippets shown below is available in CustomCollector.java class):

```
// CustomCollector.java#collectToCustomCollector

// A supplier
Supplier<StringBuilder> supplier = StringBuilder::new;
```

The next task is to create an accumulator whose job is to add up the given
instruments with a comma delimiter. An accumulator is a consumer
function, BiConsumer, the following code snippet shows the logic:

```
BiConsumer<StringBuilder, Trade> accumulator =
(sb,trade)-> sb.append(trade.getInstrument()).append(",");
```

As you can see, the accumulator is picking the instrument from each trade

141

and storing it the `StringBuilder`, appending a comma at the end.

Lastly, a combiner is needed to aggregate all the instruments stored in the `StringBuilder`. It works by concatenating the strings of intermediate results ultimately producing a final value:

```
BiConsumer<StringBuilder, StringBuilder> combiner =
  (s1, s2) -> s1.append(s2.toString());
```

As we have all the ingredients, time to call the collect method:

```
// Final step - collecting to a custom collector
StringBuilder results = trades.stream()
  .collect(supplier, accumulator, combiner);

// Output
GOOG,APPL,IBM,IBM
```

Our our own collector is capable of collecting the instruments of all the trades as a comma separated string.

We can also develop additional collectors, for example implementing the `Collector` interface and passing it to the `collect` method (remember, `stream.collect` method accepts a `Collector` implementation?). I will leave it up to you to play with the idea.

Min, Max and Average

Finding out the statistics of the stream is an important function. Luckily, there's an easy and convenient way of grabbing the *minimum*, *maximum* and *average* including *size* of the stream. Java 8 introduced a new class called `IntSummaryStatistics` which exposes all these stats in one go. See the code snippet shown below:

```
// Stats.java#summaryOfTrades

List<Trade> trades = TradeUtil.createTrades();

// fetch the summary
IntSummaryStatistics stats = trades
  .stream()
  .collect(Collectors.summarizingInt(Trade::getQuantity));

//Output
IntSummaryStatistics{count=4,sum=9200000,min=200000,
average=2300000.000000, max=4000000}
```

This time, we use a different collector by invoking `summarizingInt`. This collector does a marvellous job of creating the stream statistics when asked for. The return type is an instance of `IntSummaryStatistics` object which collates the stats.

This class encapsulates all the stats functions in one go, but sometimes we may want to have individual stats for fetching minimum or maximum values from a stream. The library provides functions such as `min`, `max`, `average` etc for this purpose, which is the subject of the next section.

Range and Stats

We learned about primitive streams earlier. They are specialised streams to avoid boxing and unboxing costs when working with primitives. They also expose functionalities in finding out minimum or maximum or average of a set of numbers. But before we explore them, it's important to get an understanding of range methods.

range Method

The `IntStream` exposes a static method called `range` for producing a stream of integers. For example, if we need to produce a continuous stream of integers from 10 to 20, we invoke `range` passing in the starting and ending point of the numbers, as demonstrated in the following segment of code:

```
// Stats.java#usingRange

// Stream of integers from 10 to 20
IntStream streamOfInts = IntStream.range(10, 20);
streamOfInts.forEach(System.out::println);

// Output
10, 11, 12,…19
```

Keep a note that the end number provided to the method (20 is not printed out to the console) will not be included in the range because the range *excludes* the end number. If we want both bounds to be included, we should use `rangeClosed` method instead of `range` method.

rangeClosed Method

If we want the range to be inclusive of both starting and ending numbers, we should use `rangeClosed` instead, as shown in the following code block:

```
// Stats.java#usingRangeClosed

IntStream streamOfInts = IntStream.rangeClosed(10, 20);
streamOfInts.forEach(s -> System.out.print(s+" "));

// Output
10, 11, 12,…20
```

Min and Max Methods

Now as we know how to prepare a stream of integers, let's see how we can find the maximum, minimum and average of the integers in the stream. It's quite straight forward, as the code snippet below shows:

```
// Stats.java#minMaxAndAverage

IntStream streamOfInts = IntStream.rangeClosed(1, 100);

OptionalInt max = streamOfInts.max();
System.out.println("Max: "+max.getAsInt());

// Output

Max: 100
```

Similarly, invoke min method on the stream to get the minimum value while average fetches the average of all elements:

```
// Stats.java#minMaxAndAverage

IntStream streamOfInts = IntStream.rangeClosed(49, 59);

// Minimum
OptionalInt min = streamOfInts.min();
System.out.println("Min: "+min.getAsInt());

//Output
Min: 49

// Average
OptionalDouble avg = streamOfInts.average();
System.out.println("Avg: "+avg.getAsDouble());

// Output
Avg: 17.5
```

Note the return type OptionalDouble when calculating average as averages are represented as floating point numbers.

Summary

In this chapter, we learned about grouping and partitioning data as well as working through examples of preparing n-dimensional grids using multi-level grouping and partitioning features. We also looked at creating our own collectors. We finally went through stream statistics using `IntSummaryStatistics` class as well as individual methods such as `min`, `max` and `average`.

14. PARALLELL PROCESSING

Multi-core machines are here, today's PCs, laptops and tablets are all built with multi-core processors. Utilising the cores effectively to speed up the computation is as essential as oil to an engine. Pre-Java 8 libraries were old and more geared for a single cpu architectures than the modern multi-core processing architectures.

Increase in the processing capabilities and arrival of the big data applications pushed Java platform to the edge. Java 8 embraced the challenges and enhanced the parallel processing techniques. This chapter deals with the details of parallel programming paradigm in Java 8.

Serial Execution

So far, we've been processing the data using streams in a serial fashion., that is, none of our programs were executed in parallel. We did not write any multi-threading code.

Beginning with Java 8, we can create a program in a parallel mode by simply invoking `parallel` method provided by the `Stream` interface! This will auto-magically run our program on multi cores, slicing and aggregating all the data.

Previous to Java 8, the *Fork and Join* framework were the best tool to write parallel processing code. Under the hood, parallel streams uses this framework so we can concentrate on business logic.

Say we have a serial stream code that calculates the total quantity by summing up all the big trade's values. we first create a `Predicate` and a `Function` which can be passed to a filter and mapper functions respectively. The following code demonstrate these two functions

```
// ParallelStreams.java#serialStream

// Filter predicate
Predicate<Trade> filterPredicate = t -> {
  System.out.printf("Id:%d  Filter:  %s:\n",t.getId(),
Thread.currentThread().getName());

  return t.isBigTrade();
};

// Map function
Function<Trade, Integer> mapFunction = t -> {
    System.out.printf("Id:%d  Mapper:%s:\n",  t.getId(),
Thread.currentThread().getName());

  return t.getQuantity();
};
```

For the sake of displaying the `Thread` info, we have added print statements to the lambda expressions so the input trade and the `Thread` are printed out. The print statements serves the purpose of identifying the executing thread. When executed, the functions will printout information as shown below:

```
// Output
Id: 2 Filter Thread: main
Id: 2 Map Thread: main
Id: 4 (Filter Thread=ForkJoinPool.commonPool-worker-2)
```

Now that we have couple of lambdas, we can wire them up during a pipeline processing:

```
Optional<Integer> sumOfTrades = trades
  .stream()
  .filter(filterPredicate)
  .map(mapFunction)
  .reduce(Integer::sum);
```

Here, we are applying a filter and a map on the stream elements. This way, we know exactly which thread is processing the element. Finally, the `reduce` method collects the quantities and accumulates them to produce a final sum.

By default, the code will execute in a serial fashion. The following output is printed to the console when we run the program:

```
// Output
Id: 1 Filter Thread: main:
Id: 2 Filter Thread: main:
Id: 2 Map Thread: main:
Id: 3 Filter Thread: main:
Id: 4 Filter Thread: main:
Id: 4 Map Thread: main:
Sum: 6000000
```

We clearly see there is only one thread (the main thread) which has been deployed for processing the elements. Although this program is running on my quad core processor machine, there's no sign of other threads being called since, by default, programs run in a serial fashion.

Before we delve into parallel processing mode, let us consider how the events are executed in the pipeline.

The first element (Id: 1) was processed by the filter, but was dropped as it did not meet the big-trade condition and hence didn't make it to mapping stage. The second trade is a big trade and hence passed the filtering criteria, moved to mapping stage and subsequently collected. Hence, you see two statements for a trade with (Id: 2) – one in the filter stage and another one in the mapping stage. The pipeline process restarts with the third element and processing go on.

Parallel Execution

Under-utilizing resources is a sin in processing data software, especially if the application is a resource hungry and data intensive. Imagine a billion trades passing through the pipeline and processing all of them *one-by-one* in a serial fashion!

How do we instruct the program to start using threads to speedup the processing without getting our hands dirty? Do we need to start building the fork/join framework infrastructure or start writing custom multi-threading code?

Fortunately Java 8 comes with all bells and whistles when it comes to parallellism. The following code is a slight modification to the serial code we had seen earlier (although the slight modification, impact is huge!):

```
trades.stream()
  .parallel()
  .filter(Trade::isBigTrade)
  .map(t -> t.getQuantity())
  .reduce(Integer::sum);
```

Invoking parallel method on the stream will simply turn the processing to a multi-core, that's as simple as it can get!

For our understanding, let's add some debug statements so we know which thread is being run. There's a handy method called peek, which simply debugs the input and prints to the console. It is an intermediate operation and mostly used for system debugging and unit testing.

So, here's the code after adding print statements:

```
// ParallellStreams.java#parallelStream

trades.stream()
  .parallel()
  .filter(Trade::isBigTrade)
  .peek(t->print("Id=%d Filter Thread Name=%s\n",
      t.getId(), Thread.currentThread().getName()))
  .map(t-> t.getQuantity())
  .peek(t->print("Mapper Thread=%s\n",
      Thread.currentThread().getName()))
  .reduce(Integer::sum);
```

Execute this program and check out the output:

```
// Output from a parallel run
Id=3 Filter Thread=main
Id=2 Filter Thread=ForkJoinPool.commonPool-worker-1
Id=4 Filter Thread=ForkJoinPool.commonPool-worker-2
Mapper Thread=ForkJoinPool.commonPool-worker-1
Mapper Thread=main
Mapper Thread=ForkJoinPool.commonPool-worker-2
Aggregate in parallel mode:9000000
```

From the above output, we can learn that various threads like worker-1 and worker-2 (which are part of Fork Join common pool) have started. Also, notice that the trades were processed in different order, which is true when parallel execution is in place. The methods such as filter, map and reduce methods will be executed on different threads according the inbuilt parallel algorithm.

Using *parallelStream* Method

There's another way of creating a parallel stream when working with collections. Collections API has a method called `parallelStream` introduced in Java 8, which returns a parallel stream, as shown below:

```
// ParallelStreams.java#collectionParallelStream

Stream<Trade> parallelStreams =
  trades.parallelStream();

parallelStreams.forEach(System.out::println);
```

The `trades.parallelStream` will create a pipeline in a parallel mode directly (rather than converting from sequential to parallel mode).

Behind The Scenes

We learned how to convert a sequential program to a parallel one. All we had to do was to invoke `parallel` method on the stream. How in the world a single method would take away the pain and suffering of working with thread safety, concurrency and parallelism? Are there any threads created, and if so, do we have control over them? How is the data split into various chunks, what is the chunk size and how is it distributed to other threads? The simple answer is that Java 8 uses fork/join framework under the wraps for achieving parallellism. We don't need to deal with chunking or sub-task slicing or job scheduling. The framework is hidden away from us. Let's learn a tad bit more about the framework and its details in Java 8.

Fork/Join Framework

In order to understand Java 8's parallelism, it is imperative to look at fork/join framework first introduced in Java 7. The fork/join framework on the high level is simple: it splits the job into sub-jobs thus exploiting the multiple cores. Each sub-job is given to a thread for processing and ultimately once the sub-jobs are completed, the final result is produced by combining all the sub-job results. This way each of the sub-job can run on a separate processor, thus utilizing all the cores.

The big advantage in Java 8 is that parallelism comes for almost with a flick of a button. We don't have to design and develop the `RecursiveTasks` or `RecursiveActions` that are part and parcel of fork/join framework. The data is automatically spilt into chunks, each chunk given to a thread and ultimately aggregated the results received from all these tasks producing the final result.

Threads

Now we know that parallel processing is carried out by using the fork/join framework, let's answer the question of how many threads are created when working with parallel programs?

The fork/join framework uses a ForkJoinPool for creating and executing tasks. A ForkJoinPool is a concrete implementation of ExecutorService which is the centre of the fork/join mechanism. One of the characteristics of this pool is that it's algorithm is based on work-stealing (a less busier thread can steal the work from a lot busier thread) function. The ForkJoinPool takes the responsibility of chunking the data into mini chunks and then executing the tasks or actions submitted to it.

> Fork/Join framework is the workhorse behind the Java 8's parallel execution feature. Java runtime takes care of most everything allowing us to concentrate on logic at hand than infrastructural jobs.

So, when we execute a parallel stream, a ForkJoinPool creates a set number of threads automatically for the job to run parallell. By default it creates as many threads as the cores.

There's a property called *parallelism* on ForkJoinPool class that would dictate the number of threads that the pool would use to execute parallel tasks. You can find out the number of threads by asking the ForkJoinPool politely:

```
// ParallelStreams.java#howManyThreads

// Create an instance of the class
ForkJoinPool fjPool = new ForkJoinPool();

// Fetch number of available/allocated threads
int allocatedThreads = fjPool.getParallelism();
System.out.println("Thread count: "+allocatedThreads);
```

By invoking the getParallelism on the pool it will return a positive integer which denotes the number of threads that are available on the machine. When I execute the above method on my quad core laptop, I get 4 as the thread count - one thread per core. However, one of them is a main thread, while the other three threads belong to ForkJoinPool common pool.

The number of threads in a common pool is one less than the available processors (`Runtime.getRuntime().availableProcessors()`) on the computer. There is a way to alter the thread count by tweaking the `java.util.concurrent.ForkJoinPool.common.parallelism` property. This property needs to be set as a vm argument, passing the required number of threads, as demonstrated below:

```
// Command line vm argument
-Djava.util.concurrent.ForkJoinPool.common.parallelism=16

// Setting programmatically
System.setProperty("java.util.concurrent.ForkJoinPool.comm
on.parallelism","16");
```

Consider the following example which demonstrates how to increase the number of threads in parallel processing:

```
// ParallellStreams.java#changeParallellism

IntStream intStream = IntStream.rangeClosed(0, 5);

// Set the parallelism property
System.setProperty("java.util.concurrent.ForkJoinPool.comm
on.parallelism", "10");

// Run the program in parallell
intStream.parallel().forEach(i -> {
  System.out.println(Thread.currentThread().getName());
});

// Output
main
ForkJoinPool.commonPool-worker-13
ForkJoinPool.commonPool-worker-9
ForkJoinPool.commonPool-worker-4
ForkJoinPool.commonPool-worker-11
ForkJoinPool.commonPool-worker-2
```

In the example above, we have an `IntStream` ranging from 0 to 5 running the `forEach` operation in parallel mode. The `forEach` here doesn't do much except printing out the thread's name that it uses. We also set the number of threads to be created using the `System` property setting. The output explains that we have six different threads (five are `ForkJoinPool`'s threads and one is the main thread) actively working on our program.

Even though I have a quad core machine, I created more threads than advised (suggested recommendation is one thread per processor), which may not be ideal. Creating more threads may sometimes be detrimental to the performance of the program as there's an overhead of context switching, lock contentions and others. The usual recommendation is to have n (or n+1 where the extra thread might be queued up, ready to jump in if needed) threads where n is the number of processors.

The next thing we need to look at is how does the data gets chopped into chunks (sub-jobs). There's a new mechanism introduced in Java 8 for chunking the data to supply to various threads called Spliterator.

Spliterator

As the names suggests Spliterator is a *splittable iterator*. It's no different from our iterator friend, except that the Spliterator will split the data into chunks for parallel processing. That is, it slices the data to create chunks that can be given to threads on different cores. A Spliterator can in turn fork a new Spliterator, too.

Fortunately, we will not have to work with Spliterators as Java 8 provides default implementations for all the collections. However, should you wish to implement one, you can, but I'm afraid we will not be discussing custom spliterator here.

Here is how the Spiliterator works: If the size of the chunk is greater than expected, the trySplit method would be invoked to spawn off another Spliterator chunk. This Spliterator in turn takes in a portion of chunk and rest will be given to another spliterator by calling trySplit again. This splitting process continues until the last part of the chunk is not divisible any more.

Usage of Parallel Streams

As easy as it may sound, parallel streams are not exactly a magic bullet for your performance problems. In fact, using parallelism in certain situations may be counter productive. Unless we analyse the case with the data you have at hand throughly, we can't conclude that parallel stream is the right fit for your purpose. Let's discuss some features that one may need to consider before introducing parallel streams to applications:

Ordering

We may have zillion cores at our disposal, but if ordering is a prime requirement, we are stuck! Maintaining order simply forces us to adopt a single-threaded model. Also, ordering data is most certainly adds to overhead. Having to have no ordering at all is a blessing but unfortunately not every one is blessed with unordered data processing requirements.

Hence, if ordering or sequencing of data is a prime importance, there's little you can achieve by parallel processing.

Data Size and Population

Data size is another factor that most developers should consider before resorting to parallel execution. Bigger size data are better candidates for parallelism, of course, other factors. Do not attempt going parallel mode when your data set is tiny weeny! There's a initial cost involved in creating threads, switching the contexts and chunking the data. Go parallel if you can offset the initial and runtime costs.

Benchmarking

Before you derive to any conclusions, we must create a benchmark tool for analysing the various factors involved in performance decision making process. One should create detailed test for checking the performance measure of both serial and parallel versions. It's not difficult to test these modes side-by-side (all you need to change is the name of the method to switch from serial to parallel execution). So measure the performance before you arrive to a conclusion.

What ever you do, make sure you create an appropriate benchmark test suite for measuring performance of parallel streams. Study the plethora of variables that come into play when parallelism is concerned.

Performance benchmarking is a subject on it's own and certainly out of scope for this book. However, there are various frameworks and tools available, so I would strongly recommend you pick one that you are comfortable with. I would suggest JMH (http://openjdk.java.net/projects/code-tools/jmh) from Java guys, the in-depth benchmarking tool.

Simplified Example

For completeness, let's create a very simplified example that would check the run times both in serial and parallel modes. The following code snippet is demonstrating time taken for running an aggregation on set of trades in a sequential mode:

```
// PerformanceExample.java#sequentialMode

Instant start = Instant.now();

// Sequential mode
// use trades.stream.parallel() for parallel mode
trades.stream()
  .map(Trade::getQuantity)
  .reduce(Integer::sum);

Instant end = Instant.now();

Duration d = Duration.between(start, end);
System.out.printf("%s %d %s" , "Aggregating trades took ",
d.toMillis()," ms in sequential mode\n ");

// Output
Aggregating trades took  91  ms in seqential mode
```

We use the reduction operation to sum up the total trades in a sequential fashion. On my machine it took about 91ms for processing handful of trades. This test is a crude performance test, but it provides a basic understanding of performance that can used for selecting a sequential or a parallel execution.

In order to check the performance in parallel mode, use the same code except changing the pipeline to a parallel execution by invoking `parallel` method on the stream. When I run the program on my machine, I got this output:

```
Aggregating trades took 91  ms in sequential mode
Aggregating trades took 14  ms in parallel mode
```

However, the above result should not be the only factor to consider, there are other issues that you need to consider before selecting a mode of computation. As I mentioned earlier, you must create your own performance criteria and perhaps pick up an off-the shelf tool like JMH to evaluate them.

Summary

In this chapter, we looked at the the serial and parallel streams, browsed through the mechanics of thread creation as well as the understanding the fork/join framework's role in parallel executions. We looked at the need for the benchmarking parallel programs and testing them thoroughly before leaning towards parallel execution.

ALSO FROM THE AUTHOR

CPSIA information can be obtained
at www.ICGtesting.com
Printed in the USA
LVOW04s2128020316

477486LV00026B/1314/P